THE FAMILY BOOK OF FUN

Other books by

Shirley and Monroe Paxman

FAMILY NIGHT FUN

PARTY PATTERNS

THE FAMILY BOOK OF FUN

by

Shirley Brockbank Paxman
and Monroe J. Paxman

GRAMERCY PUBLISHING COMPANY • NEW YORK

ACKNOWLEDGMENT is gratefully made for permission to quote from *This Week* Magazine and from *Children's Friend*. Thanks are due also to those in the fields of education, recreation and youth guidance—as well as to the wonderful families we know—whose activities have been a rich source for us in gathering the materials for this book.

Library of Congress Catalog Number 62-10552

This edition published by Gramercy Publishing Co., a division of Crown Publishers, Inc., by arrangement with Prentice-Hall, Inc.
(A)

Printed in the United States of America

Introduction

We believe wholeheartedly that families should have fun. But we believe fun can have a purpose. Since the publication of *Family Night Fun* we have received countless suggestions for ways in which families *can* have fun with a purpose. This book is full of those ideas. Just reading it won't make you any happier, of course, but if you read it, think about it, and do something about what it suggests, then it will really add to the fullness of your family life. How? By showing ways in which you can enrich the hours when you are together as a family, by showing you that these hours can be the most rewarding, delightful and happiest hours you will ever spend. Many of the activities here are suitable for a family hour and all of them are planned with family relationships in mind.

We do not, of course, imply that the simple addition of a regular program of activity could in any way automatically solve all the complex problems facing modern families. Still, among those who do have such a program the real results indicate that something wonderful happens to families who spend regular hours together in goodnatured activities with a purpose beyond the fun itself.

This book is our contribution to that "something wonderful" in your family life.

Contents

1.

Traditions Need Beginnings

ToDAY's FAMILIES LIVE IN SUCH A BUSY CENTRIFUGAL world. Fathers work long hours in order to earn the money necessary to support a family. Many mothers also work outside the home in order to ease the economic situation. Those mothers who do not work are kept busy trying to meet the demanding schedules of the home, PTA, clubs, church, and community. Children certainly are on the go, and must work hard to keep up with the pressures of their school, athletic, and social life.

All in all, mothers, fathers, and children are spending more and more time away from home. More and more functions are being planned outside the home by recreational, church, school, and other organizations. It is true that many of these organizations are worthy ones and their programs desirable, but still these activities are not the answer to the need for family unity that is reflected in our high rates of divorce and juvenile delinquency.

Develop Skills at Home

While we are the first to admit that many of these programs are desirable and often necessary for the sake of the child and the parent, it would be well if the child could be taught the beauties of nature, the joy of a job well done, and the requirements for good sportsmanship within the circle of his own family.

11

Today's tendency is for parents to let organizations take over the responsibility of rearing the children. Ambitious and conscientious parents everywhere are flocking to enroll their offspring in every conceivable type of program—dancing, music lessons, little league, cub scouting, foreign languages, little theater, swimming, camping, tennis, and even chess lessons.

Why is it that parents today work hard and long to provide material things for their children and yet there are more children hungry for love, sympathy and understanding than for food? In a day when material possessions are emphasized, let us keep in mind that the most desirable and worthwhile gifts cost nothing. The least costly but most priceless gifts that parents can give their children are the gifts of love shared, of problems faced together as a cohesive unit, the gifts of understanding and concern, of laughter and fun. None of these costs anything in terms of dollars and cents. A friendly pillow fight at bedtime, a belly flop on a sled, a walk through colorful leaves, iceskating under the stars—none of these costs money but each is worth more in rich memories than the most expensive gift. These memories are the gifts which bring back a long-lost delight in later years when childhood has passed and the home is quiet.

Traditions Build Happiness

Dr. James H. Bossard, Sociology Professor at the University of Pennsylvania, says that family traditions are a key to family happiness. In a study he made, he found that families without these binding traditions are more likely to fall apart than families with them.

Children enjoy rituals most of all, but parents too can reap the pleasures that evolve from establishing traditions. Rituals help children to grow and develop by giving them a sense of security and vivid memories which they will treasure for a lifetime. Even the practice of doing something over and over again can bring satisfaction, as every parent knows who looks forward to Christmas when the role of family traditions becomes most important. In fact, in many families most traditions are centered around holidays and birthdays. But traditions needn't stop there!

Most families can and many families do start rituals or traditions that are uniquely their own. They do it without thinking about it or planning it because this is the way most traditions begin. They just happen! A family finds something so pleasant to do that they want to do it over and over again in a certain way. Many of your family activities can blossom into traditions with just a little encouragement. The gingerbread man baked on a Saturday afternoon, the delicious Lily Cakes served on each Easter Sunday, the trip down the river on a summer afternoon floating on inflated inner tubes, the search for wood violets in the early spring, a potato roast in the bonfire made from the first autumn leaf-raking project, the ice cream made from the first snow of winter, a picnic supper on midsummer's eve—of such small things are traditions made!

It isn't so much what you do that is important, but that you *do* it!

One of our cherished traditions began with an autumn ride through the mountains to see the brilliant array of colors nature had provided. We packed a picnic lunch and invited another family to join us. Each autumn since then both families have loaded picnic hampers, cameras, dogs, footballs, and children into their cars and gone off to spend an exhilarating day in the brilliantly hued woods.

Another family tradition began when our oldest boy, then five, took part in a program at church one Sunday evening. After the service we honored him by stopping at a local ice cream parlor for a treat. This has become a popular tradition in our family that has been repeated through the years. Whenever any member of the family performs, either by giving a talk, playing a musical number, or singing on a program, the entire family goes to the ice cream store for a treat. In this small way we convey the love and pride we feel in their accomplishments. We must admit that the thought of a luscious banana split or ice cream sundae is an added incentive that increases the children's willingness to perform when asked!

Enjoy a Family Hour

Our family hour is one of the most rewarding and dearest family traditions we have. This is a certain time set aside each week when we get together to spend an hour or two in worthwhile pursuits. Sometimes we just have fun. Other times we try to accomplish something that will improve our family life together. Sometimes we discuss serious things. Other times we relax and play games. These hours we spend together, inviolate from outside distractions, are the happiest hours of all. Our family hours bring us close together in a warm relationship; they strengthen the bonds between members of the family and help bridge the gap between parents and children by offering an opportunity to talk with each other about hopes, problems, and plans in a friendly atmosphere. These hours strengthen and develop qualities of love through the help we give each other. They make home life more attractive and satisfying by giving voice to the joy of living with each other.

Over the years we have found many other families who are completely converted to the idea of a regular family night or family hour. While the basic ingredients of good fun and good fellowship are the same in every family, still the family hour itself takes on different forms in different families. For example, one family calls its family night "Whoopee" night. On this evening the whole family hurries through washing the dishes and cleaning the kitchen. Then, if it is show night, there follows a variety of stunts and dramatics. On story night, favorite stories are told or dramatized. On game night various table games are played, or it might be action games. At least once a month they try to learn a new game. Often they make the necessary equipment for the game from things found around the house.

Another family has a different version of family night. They change the usual pattern and add interest by dividing the hour into ten or fifteen minute periods. Then each member decides how he wants the family to spend his period of time. One child may want to play a game, another may want to spend it in group singing, another may want to discuss something of special interest. Everyone agrees to follow the wishes of the person in charge of that particular period. Since this family is large, everyone may not get a chance to have a choice in one evening but the idea is repeated another time so everyone gets a turn.

Spiritual and Cultural Joy

In the family hour, we have found an increase in spiritual and cultural joy that has intensified our relationship and responsibility to God, our family, our community, and our country. Through the family hour, we have increased our knowledge of good books, good music, good drama, good citizenship, the world around us, the sky above us, and the earth beneath us. We have increased our appreciation for other people, races, and religions. We have learned the pleasure of play and the worthiness of work. We have studied the scriptures and discussed the main principles of successful living, strengthening our belief in God and confirming our faith in Him. We have discussed the principles of freedom and the responsibilities inherent in living in a free land. Above all, we learn one of the greatest secrets of successful living—"to live in the present and create memories for the future."

2.

Seriously Speaking

Pɴᴀʀᴇɴᴛᴀʟ ɪɴꜱᴛʀᴜᴄᴛɪᴏɴ ɪɴ ʟɪғᴇ'ꜱ ᴘʀᴏʙʟᴇᴍꜱ ɪꜱ ᴏɴᴇ ᴏғ ᴛʜᴇ greatest needs of the home today. While parents desire to do only what is best for their children, they often hesitate or shy away from instructing them in proper spiritual and material values and in the special problems that confront growing boys and girls—such as sex, relating to other young people, dating, driving a car, and choosing good companions in marriage.

For us, one of the greatest advantages of having a regular home night or family hour is that it provides the setting for instructions of this kind. Parents and children, relaxed and unified in this quiet hour of sharing, can establish a rapport that will encourage confidence.

Many of the problems facing families, and specifically the children, can be approached at this time by storytelling, play-acting and discussions. There are many good stories that can be used to illustrate fine character traits. The Bible, of course, is one nearly inexhaustible source, and others are found in the exemplary lives of great men and women. Parents would do well to choose some of these stories for family hour programs.

For example, tell a story of honesty, and then discuss what honesty means in terms of the children's ages and experience. Make the discussion personal and graphic so they will fully understand. Discuss as a family what it means to be honest. Make a list of the different types of honesty, such as speaking the truth, not taking things that belong to others, returning what you borrow, not cheating, not deceiving, taking blame for what you do, never taking credit for someone else's work, always doing one's share, always keeping promises.

Another character trait subject is loyalty. Perhaps you would enjoy reviewing the stories of famous people who have been loyal to their ideals. Childcraft's volume of *Great Men and Famous Deeds* has many beautifully written stories about characters in history and in the Bible who were stalwart and loyal to their people, their country, their family, or their ideals. Any of these stories could be retold or dramatized by the family members. The story of Benedict Arnold is a graphic illustration of what happens to people who are disloyal. The story of Joseph and his brothers in the Old Testament is another good one.

Fault-finding is another subject that would be profitable to discuss during your family hour. Each day for a week family members could take turns keeping a record of the times each one is found finding fault or criticizing someone else. During family hour discuss the list and what can be done to improve the attitude of each member. Set a goal of *not* finding fault and work on it as a project.

FAMILY WORSHIP

Spiritual life begins in the home, and every home should be dedicated to divine worship, whatever the faith or creed practiced. Families need daily devotion in the home in order to strengthen the family and protect it against undesirable influences. One of the strongest expressions given in the Old Testament was made by Joshua when he said, "Choose you this day whom ye will serve; but as for me and my house, we will serve the Lord." Families today can profit by accepting a similar challenge.

Children should be taught the goodness of God, the family's dependence on Him, the desire to do His will. They should learn to express thanks to God for His many blessings. It is within the environs of the home that children learn respect for and appreciation of a belief in God and a religious creed. Whatever practices and principles of religion the family believes in, these concepts should be taught with love, devotion and sincerity.

An ancient Persian quotation taken from their sacred books says, "If you would be holy, instruct your children, because all good acts they perform will be imputed unto you."

Family Prayer

Families benefit by establishing the traditions of family prayers, individual prayers, the old-fashioned practice of daily devotion in the home, singing hymns, and the reading of scriptures. Happiness results when parents build testimonies to God in the hearts of their children. The family is strengthened and fortified because love and obedience flourish more readily in a spiritual environment.

Nearly all religious families incorporate into their way of worship the practice of saying grace at mealtimes; and with more families going to church then ever before, this beautiful and expressive custom is more widely practiced. If your family is used to *saying* grace at mealtimes, you might like to try *singing* some of the simple well-known prayers with your family. It is a delightful way to start the mealtime or the family hour. One of the most familiar graces is the following:

Be present at our table, Lord,
Be here and everywhere adored.
These mercies bless, and grant that we
May feast in paradise with thee. Amen.

You can set this simple grace to music by singing it to the tune of the Doxology or "Sweet Genevieve." You might like to try singing some of your favorite prayers by joining them to simple familiar tunes.

Teaching Proper Values

There is a rising feeling among many parents that there has been an overemphasis on the *importance* of money. Many parents feel that they should reduce the emphasis on money and substitute other values in its place. As one discerning parent said, "I would like my children to have more ambition and less acquisition."

Too often parents themselves are responsible for the attitude that money or the dollar sign is the basis for evaluating a person's success in life. Children hearing parents say, "The Hales are a lovely couple and very well to do," or "He's really got it made," tend to think that money is the standard criterion for judging a person's worth.

Character, Not Cash

The family hour is a good time to discuss what constitutes good taste, what makes a person cultured, what relationship opulence has to standards of good taste, whether ostentation is desirable, if money should influence your judgment of people, if you should cultivate friends for what they can do for you or because you genuinely like them, whether you should support causes because of your belief in the cause or because it is popular or fashionable, if it is easier to take guests to a restaurant or club for lunch than to entertain them at home. These questions could be discussed by the parents and children, with the parents guiding the discussion to encourage the proper emphasis on particular values.

As a family, have a project of listing all the "priceless" experiences you have had or plan to have that are not "costly." You might start out with a firelight to dream by, archy and mehitabel to laugh with, popcorn to munch, and good music to listen to. Surely not even costly worldly goods could provide more happiness than the appreciation of these simple things.

If you can cultivate and encourage your children to create their own fun and develop family projects from their own efforts and creativity, you will have gone a long way in establishing a balanced sense of values. Children should be taught early in life that a person's worth should be measured by *character* and not *cash*, and that *character* is more important in a home than *conveniences*. If you encourage making cookies or having a backyard barbeque in preference to going to the store and buying treats, if you can enjoy a play from general admission seats just as well as from box seats, if you turn down the boat you can't afford but want because all your friends have one, you will be helping your children develop a yardstick for measuring real worth in material things as well as in people. And in this day of materialism and the bank account, this is no small achievement!

"Rediscovery of the Private Self"

In every large family there is a tendency to bunch activities and people together. "Togetherness" is charming and delightful in many respects but it can be suffocating if all activities are group activities.

As Mrs. Bonaro Overstreet explains in her "Rediscovery of the Private Self," every individual needs some time to himself. And each child especially needs some time alone with a parent. The lack of competition, not having to share the parent's attention with others, gives a child a real sense of belonging and the knowledge that he is loved for his own particular self, not because he is a part of the group.

In one family of seven children, the parents make a point of singling out just one child to do something special with. The father often asks one child to accompany him on business trips. Sometimes they take an all-day trip by car, sometimes it is a week-end jaunt. Occasionally they travel by air. While Dad conducts his business the child is free to go swimming, sight-seeing, or read a good book. As soon as Dad is through work, they form a twosome for dinner, a movie, or a swim, and then back to the hotel for a good night's sleep. When the mother goes on a shopping trip to the city, she makes it a special occasion by taking one daughter with her for the day. They have lunch at a nice restaurant, go on a shopping tour through the lovely shops, and maybe have time for a matinee and a late sundae before going home. A feeling of companionship and closeness results from this special afternoon away from the others. It is exciting to see how one child blossoms when the attention is solely on *him*. Such a day is a lovely talisman to carry back to the family group again and acts as a buffer against the normal competition of everyday family living.

If your child is young, together you can plan to do something he would particularly enjoy, such as a visit to the duck pond in the park, a trip to a pet shop, or seeing a puppet-show. As the child grows older, the choices will broaden. Then a trip to the library, a bike ride, or a museum visit will be of interest.

Every Saturday since his daughter was twelve one father has taken her to lunch at a pleasant restaurant and afterwards to a football game, movie, or play. On these outings father and daughter never include anyone else, because they discuss her social and school problems. This close association makes it easier to be aware of the activities and interests of children, since they are naturally away from home more and more as they grow older.

Let's Learn to Work

In most families lots of activities are planned to create fun but we realize that parents who are perennial pals can be a pain in the neck. There are times when dignity and authority are absolutely necessary in the family relationship, and we encourage this type of training. Just as families need to play together, so do they need to work together. Many skills can be taught in the home that will be a source of joy and accomplishment to the children in later life. Mother should teach her daughters to cook, sew, and keep house. Dad should teach his sons how to do simple electrical repairs and handle woodworking tools as well as golf clubs!

Many work projects will benefit the entire family and can be done as family projects, such as building a barbeque pit, painting the play room, laying a brick wall, or installing an outdoor shower. The project can be something as involved as building a week-end retreat in the woods, finishing the basement, or building a boat. Or it can be as simple as repairing the wheel on a toy wagon, building a tree house, or fixing the screen door.

A child's attitude toward work will be a reflection of his parents' attitude. It is a wise parent who teaches his children that work is part of life, that sometimes work must be done whether we like the job or not, and that work well done brings many deep and lasting rewards.

Young children can be taught to do simple household jobs such as dusting, emptying wastebaskets, setting the table, clearing dishes, running errands, watering house plants, and sweeping the sidewalks. If possible, they should be given jobs worth doing rather than "busy work." Chores shouldn't be used as punishment unless they serve a specific purpose. An orderly system of assigning chores should be followed so no child feels "picked on," and some supervision or assistance should be given until the child learns the best way to do a particular job. Praise is a must for a job well done.

Many families have devised novel systems for following through on work assignments. Some families use the family bulletin board to list the various projects. A chart is posted on the board with the name of each child and his specific duty is listed. When the job is finished, the project is checked off. Still another family uses a card file, with the cards posted on the bulletin board and then removed when the work is done.

One resourceful mother uses signs to help the work along. She has two signs, one painted "Please" and the other "Thank you." The sign saying "Please" is left on an unmade bed, an untidy chest of drawers, an uncleaned tub. The "Thank you" sign is posted in its place, when the child finishes the job. This eliminates nagging and is a polite reminder to get the job done. In another home when coats are carelessly dropped on a chair after school, a "No Parking" sign is used. On the doorknobs of the front and back doors signs hang saying "Don't Bang Me, Please!" Near the back doormat is the sign "Are Your Shoes Clean?" Near the bathroom and hall light switches are signs saying "Are you through with the light?" The tone of the signs is kept light and good-natured and family cooperation is excellent.

One mother with a large family made the rule that each Saturday work assignment *must* be finished before the child could have lunch. The children all agreed but it didn't work out as simply as it sounded. She found various children fixing their lunches as late as three and four o'clock in the afternoon. Using one of the prerogatives of a parent, she amended the rule to say "No lunch *at all* if work isn't done by noon!"

This mother had learned one of the most important rules of being a parent—that of being flexible. Often the rules in a family must be changed to meet the situation. Otherwise parents become frustrated in the constant battle to stay top man on the family totem pole.

Consider the following list of rules set up by one mother who lost the battle! She acknowledges gracefully that a sense of humor helps. It may help you to gain perspective and to use the light-touch when you face similar situations. She calls it her "Strategic Retreat."

On Neatness

1. Children are to put away their own things.
2. Children must help Mother put away their things.
3. After Mother has put away their things, they are not to complain that she messed everything up.

On Eating Between Meals

1. Children are never to eat between meals.
2. Only fruit or milk between meals.
3. When they eat candy between meals, they must brush their teeth.

On Mealtime

1. Children must clean their plate.
2. No dessert for those who don't.
3. Absolutely NO SECOND dessert!

On Bedtime

1. Eight o'clock sharp.
2. Not one minute past 8:30.
3. Children who fall asleep while staying up late will not be carried to bed.
4. Unless they won't wake up.

On Playing in the Living Room

1. Children must not play with glue or paint in the living room.
2. When playing with glue or paint in the living room, they must spread a newspaper to catch spills.
3. Must say "I'm sorry" when they don't spread a paper and spill glue or paint on the living room rug.

On Evening Guests

1. Children must not get out of bed when guests arrive.
2. May get up only to say hello.
3. Must say goodbye nicely as guests depart.

On Watching TV

1. Children shall not watch scary TV programs.
2. After watching scary programs, they cannot come in to sleep with parents.
3. Children who must sleep with parents after a scary program cannot bring the dog to bed with them.
4. Oh, well. . . .

That's her plan, and it works. She's almost sure to be obeyed somewhere along the line.

In place of the bulletin board or mail boxes, one family used an old renovated chest of drawers to good advantage. Each child has a drawer with his name painted on it, and one extra drawer is marked "Family." Into each child's drawer goes anything that might be of interest to the owner, found and put there by any member of the family. The drawer marked "Family" holds games, puzzles, quizzes, feature articles of interest, and such. The 8-year-old's drawer has dividers and holds stamps, rocks, fossils, pictures for collections, and scraps of wood for building things. The 4-year-old gets colored pictures, empty spools, small cardboard boxes, paper, crayons, and other interesting items.

Help Children Develop Good Study Habits

The work habits developed by a child at home will carry over into his school work, especially if he has been taught to accept assignments cheerfully, to get the job done without too much "goofing off," and to not be satisfied with less than his best effort. Any teacher or educator can tell you that the encouragement and standards set by the home are prime factors in a child's achieving success in school work. The importance of the attitude at home toward learning cannot be emphasized enough.

A recent survey of four hundred famous and successful people in all fields of endeavor indicated that one of the two factors every successful person had in common with every other was that education was stressed and emphasized in the home. The other factor was that one or the other parent *insisted* on excellence in performance. In other words, they required a great deal of the child, even to the point of "pushing."

One couple, anxious for their children to go to college and concerned with the rising expense of a college education, put the problem before their family of five during a family council. Out of their discussion arose the decision for each of the members, including the three children (ages 9 to 16), to contribute 5 per cent of his net yearly income to a Family Education Fund. Eventually this money can be used by any member in the pursuit of higher education, but in the meantime the fund has provided other educational resources. It has financed a university extension course in art, trips to museums, books, and magazines. Over and above these present day benefits, the fund provides a sense of security and a sense of responsibility to the entire family. They are sure their goal will be achieved because they are preparing for it now.

You might want to evaluate the goals you are setting for your children by examining the attitude you reflect toward learning and the study habits you require and help develop in them. It would be well to spend a family hour discussing these things.

Better study habits and attitudes can be developed if children learn a few basic skills such as how to study, how to read for greater meaning, how to prepare for an exam, and how to take an examination. Excellent guides to better study habits and increasing the efficiency of a student can be found in libraries or school counseling services.

3.

Celebrations in Season

As A FAMILY PROJECT, MAKE A LARGE CALENDAR EACH month and fill in all the important events that occur during the month. This calendar will give you many ideas for family night programs. You might want to spend future family hours studying the life of some famous person, or you might wish to commemorate some historical event. The calendar will remind you that it's time for winding the Maypole, to go nut hunting, or to bake a birthday cake for a friend.

Holidays

It's lots of fun to go through the year and mark down special events and anniversaries to be celebrated each month. Our book *Family Night Fun* devotes many pages to month by month suggestions for family fun appropriate to each month and season of the year. Here are a few additional suggestions. February, for example, can feature an Abe Lincoln play and a Lincoln log dessert made of jelly roll topped with chocolate frosting or chocolate whipped cream. A Washington birthday dessert can be made from a cake decorated with pink frosting topped with maraschino cherries in clusters of three. Valentine bookmarks, cut from red felt or construction paper hearts, to clip on book pages are fun to make. Other February activities to be noted are Heart Fund Sunday and the Penny Parade fund drive for the Children's Hospital.

Try having a Family Clean-up in March. If your yard looks a little dog-eared, here's a chance to clean it up and have fun at the same time. Everyone can pitch in and pick up paper, pull weeds, rake and cut lawns, and gather up the winter's accumulation of debris. The debris is all gathered into a big bonfire and as it dies down supper can be cooked on the embers—hot dogs and baked potatoes or roasting ears wrapped in aluminum foil, served with pop, and then fruit and brownies for dessert.

How about First Flower of Spring Day, when you make a great to-do about the signs of returning spring? This could be a day to abandon work and go wandering through the countryside looking for signs of spring—the first snowflower, crocus, or wood violet.

We all have our own Memorial Days, the anniversaries of the deaths of those dear to us. And though they are not marked down on your calendar, they are written indelibly on your heart; it is in your heart that you observe them in your own way.

You might celebrate Flag Day, June 14th, by making covers out of muslin or heavy cloth to store and keep your flags clean. You might try a family project in which Mother and the girls sew the sock-like flag covers, while Dad and the boys make flag stands for displaying the flags on all legal holidays. Some neighborhoods make it a project for every home to fly the Stars and Stripes on holidays, but many other Americans are complacent and neglectful about showing patriotism by displaying the flag. Your family might encourage your neighborhood by setting a good example. This activity would also be appropriate for the Fourth of July.

Fall Favorites

In the fall we have Columbus Day, National Education Week (why not invite your children's teachers to dinner?), and United Nations Day.

Emphasize the importance of United Nations Day by serving an international menu for your family dinner. You don't need to be an expert to prepare many of the favorite foods of other lands. In fact, the United States Committee for the United Nations has prepared a booklet, "Favorite Recipes from the United Nations," that makes cooking foreign foods an exciting and easy adventure. Write to the Committee for the United Nations, 816 Twenty-first Street N.W., Washington, D. C. Most of the recipes can be prepared from foods found in our grocery stores. A typical menu might be:

Borsch

Roast Duck à la France	Guatamalan Arroz (Rice)
Uruguayan String Beans	American Cranberry Sauce
Spanish Olives	Italian Bread

Danish Ablekage

| Salted English Walnuts | Brazilian Chocolate |

Set the stage for your dinner by telling the children, or having them tell *you*, something about the United Nations and the member countries. You can get a small box of miniature flags from United Nations Building, New York, or from the Committee for the United Nations, listed above. The flags will make a gay table setting either arranged colorfully down the center of the table or used as place cards.

Fall also means Halloween. And to one family Halloween means a long drive in the country to find fat pumpkins and corn stalks. It means getting out old familiar costumes or concocting new ones and everyone dressing up including father and mother.

On the other hand, there is the "First Snow of the Season" day. This is a stay-at-home day when you sit around the fire and outline the projects you want to accomplish in the snowbound days ahead. Maybe you'll resolve to refinish the old walnut chest in the basement or enroll in a home study course in art appreciation. Maybe you'll wallpaper the guest room. It's going to be a long winter, and with all those weeks and months ahead, great things can be accomplished.

National Be-Kind-to-Mary Week

There are many national weeks already listed on the calendar or in the newspaper, and you'll want to enrich your family night program by adapting some of them to your calendar. If you find that some weeks like "National Pickle Week" don't fit your needs or interests, then make up "National Weeks" of your own. For example, one of our most successful "weeks" was observed when Mary, our 4-year-old, felt neglected as children often do. She began going around with a long, sad face and in a sad voice frequently stated, "Nobody in this family likes me. You don't like the way I talk, you don't like the way I color, you don't like anything I do!" Of course, we *did* like her very much, but in the rush of activities she felt neglected. So on our next family night we decided to have a "National-Be-Kind-to-Mary Week." Signs, embellished with hearts and flowers, were hung on the bulletin board stating that it was "National Be-Kind-to-Mary Week." All during that week members of the family concentrated on being especially kind, loving, and considerate to Mary. Each child did some extra little favor to make her happy. At the end of the week Mary was blossoming with all the attention and she surely knew that we all *did* love her very much.

One lovely lady we know celebrates "Gift Week." She picks an unlikely week, not remarkable in any way, say the first week of August. During this week she gives presents to others for no reason at all except that she wants to. They are usually inexpensive, perhaps something the recipient would love to have but wouldn't think of buying for herself. The gifts are wrapped in beautiful paper and ribbon but have no card. She feels that the point of the gift would be lost if the recipient knew the source of the gift and felt indebted. It is enough for her to know they have been made happy.

Your family will probably think of many more "weeks" you'd enjoy celebrating during the year.

Happy Birthday to You

Birthdays should be red-letter days on your calendar and many of the traditional things you do as a family to celebrate them should be noted. Birthdays have inspired numerous family customs. One father has a tradition of giving his children a silver dollar for each year on their birthdays. Another father gives each teen-ager a key to the family car when he turns 16, while still another father we know makes giant popcorn balls and hides small birthday presents inside. How the children love this treat and the surprises they find hidden in the center! A tradition in another home centers around the custom of writing funny jingles to go with each birthday present. You can imagine the shouts of laughter some of those masterpieces provoke!

A delightful custom in a family with small children has been followed over the years. The birthday child is honored at the dinner hour with a little ceremony. Crêpe paper hats and snappers as well as gaily wrapped presents decorate the place of honor as the family recites:

Something so lovely has happened today,
Guess what it is?
It's Mary's birthday!
Won't you come, Mary, and choose a bright bow
For the back of your chair,
It's your birthday you know.
And here is a cake, with bright candles too.
We'll sing one and all, Happy Birthday to you.
Mary is five, five years today
Now she may stand and decide how she may
Help somebody else to be happy and gay.

On our calendar we write down the birthdays of all our friends from nine to ninety. When their day arrives we have a family tradition of baking a birthday cake and painting a huge "Happy Birthday" sign. Taking our guitar, we all go off to serenade the honoree. This little ceremony doesn't take much time and is worth every minute of it when we see the happiness on the face of the person being honored. It is nearly always a surprise to them and a real joy to us as the children learn thoughtfulness and the pleasure of doing something for others.

A delightful switch from the usual gift was started in one family upon the birth of a new relative. They decided to present their congratulatory gift to the child's father. They have had many occasions since then to give this unusual gift. They make a drawstring bag of white muslin or duck and stencil "Papa's Pack" on the outside. The bag is then filled with individually wrapped gifts such as a plastic sheet, baby spoon, baby lotion, bibs, plug-in night light, pins, rubber pants, a congratulatory card, aspirins for Papa, and a bank book made out in the baby's name with a starting deposit. The proud father really welcomes such a gift.

Give Gifts of Time and Talents

One family whose income is limited has found a joyful substitute for birthday gift giving. Instead of buying gifts they can ill afford, they give gifts of service. And they have found many gifts that have value beyond what money can buy. They share their time and talents with others by making presents of gift certificates made out for such things as baby sitting, three hours of sewing, a bowl of home-grown peas, reading to someone who is ill, doing errands for a shut-in, and so on. If you are wondering about a gift for someone, follow this example. Use your imagination and give of your time and talents!

One family who has always made a great fuss over the birthdays of its members, including the dog, added a new note to birthday celebrations. They pooled resources and honored their home with a birthday gift. The first year, budgets being low, they concentrated on repairing and refurbishing their window blinds. Another year a new spice shelf adorned the kitchen wall, made by one of the boys in an industrial arts class at school. A remodeling job on the fireplace was the gift of another year. A set of andirons from Mother and a pair of planters for the mantel from two of the children combined to give the house a fresh and festive touch.

4.

"But Once a Year"

CHRISTMAS BEGAN WITH A FAMILY. THAT'S WHY IT HAS such a hold on our hearts, why we try to give our children memories of home and Christmas that they will always treasure. Everybody loves the feeling that comes at Christmastime when the children say "remember the year . . ." and look forward with eager anticipation to the traditions that have become honored over the years. Most families have beautiful "we do it every year" activities which they lovingly bring out each Christmas with the box of ornaments. And like the ornaments, perhaps a few traditions are time-worn, have lost their glow and need to be replaced with bright new ones. If so, your family might consider adopting some of the suggestions in this chapter.

The cornerstone of Christmas should be the Church, for there the very essence of the holiday is to be found. The Faith, the Love, and the Hope all began with that Miracle without which the message "Peace on Earth" would be meaningless and false. No matter which church your family attends, it should become an important part of your Christmas activities. In this day it is too often Santa in his sleigh who supplants the Christ child in his cradle, and in the dazzle of Christmas lights we lose sight of His star. Do not let your family miss any part of the relationship of the Christ, the Church, and

Christmas for it is in the solemn atmosphere of your house of worship that you will come closest to the true spirit of the season.

We have made the tie between church and home more than a perfunctory one in a simple tradition that brings seasonal joy to us and fellow worshipers. For many years our chapel was decorated at Christmastime only with a Christmas tree draped in tinsel and bubble lights. As we sang the simple Christmas hymns and heard the story of His birth, we wondered about the relationship of the Christmas tree to His house. It seemed incongruous as a setting for His Sacrament. Taking courage, we asked the Bishop if we might have the responsibility of decorating the church for the coming Christmas. He kindly gave consent. So, joining together with another family, we planned decorations for the chapel which we felt would be in keeping with Christ's teachings. We decided to use only those decorations that were created naturally in His beautiful world. These, we felt, were more fitting than the bubbling artificial lights and shimmering tinsel on the Christmas tree.

The day before Christmas our two families gathered together armloads of greens, pine cones, and poinsettias and took them to the church. We started decorating by hanging lovely wreaths over the entrance way to give welcome greetings to the worshipers as they entered the church. Next we hung large wreaths made of evergreens and berries in each window and banked the windowsills with fragrant boughs of balsam, cedar, spruce, and fir, with pine cones clustered among the greens. As a *pièce de résistance* a huge six foot wreath was hung over the organ grill at the front of the chapel.

While the fathers balanced precariously at the tops of tall ladders to hang the wreaths, the children were kept busy helping the mothers cut and bind branches of evergreens to adorn the pulpit and the balcony. Then the pulpit and organ were decked with beautiful red poinsettias, so colorful and exalting that they seemed to shout glad hosannas.

When all was finished we gathered up the twine, cutters, leftover greens and bits of red ribbon and walked to the back of the church to survey our handiwork. What a sense of joy and satisfaction came over us all, the children especially, as we lingered a moment in that beautiful fragrant Christmas setting. A deep feeling of reverence overcame us as we felt the peace and serenity of His spirit.

Later that afternoon, as we hurried around home busily finishing those exciting last minute preparations, the telephone rang. It was the church organist calling. With tears in her voice she said, "I just had to call and tell you what a wonderful surprise it was when I walked into the chapel and was greeted by that delicious piney fragrance and those beautiful decorations. I have never seen the church look so lovely. I was overcome with emotion, and I wanted you to know how beautiful it looks and thank you and your family for your thoughtfulness." The next morning as other members of the congregation came into the church for the Christmas Service, we were so happy that we had had a part in bringing joy to others on this wondrous day. Surely this was the spirit of Christmas!

The family that joins forces to make much of its own Christmas happiness is investing in future memories. Evenings spent around the dining room table block-printing Christmas wrapping-paper or addressing cards; hours spent stringing popcorn by the yard or creating ornaments from odds and ends around the house; afternoons in the kitchen baking cookies, cracking nuts, making candy; evenings in the basement sawing, hammering, painting a rocking horse for David, a doll house for Annette; all of these add up to years of happy afterthoughts as each Christmas season recalls the joys of time well spent together.

Christmas Gifts of Self

In our family in the weeks before Christmas each of the younger children is given a day to go Christmas shopping with Mother or Dad, just the two of them. The child is free to wander up and down aisles to choose presents for his friends and family. Each child has his own money, saved all year from gifts, birthdays, and allowances. The first stop made is at the bank and the allotted amount is withdrawn. This in itself is a dignified and impressive event! Then off we go to the stores to look at all the exciting displays in the thrilling world of Christmas shops. Children deserve a special time to Christmas shop by themselves. A day downtown allows them to gaze at store windows and to linger long over choices, to decide whether to get John the handsome pocket knife for 39¢, or the billfold for 69¢. It is a time when they don't hear, "Hurry, hurry, come on now!" not even once. The joy is enhanced for the four-year-old by taking a quarter from his own coin purse or pocket and handing it to the girl at the counter. These gifts, carefully chosen with tender, loving care, mean much more to the child than a $3.00 gift an adult might select for him to give.

When the children get older they are encouraged to do their own shopping with money earned from various jobs. They usually go it alone or in pairs with another older brother or sister. What pride they feel as they go forth, enormously rich with the proceeds from their first paper route or a baby sitting job. What secretive excitement as they come home and hurry to their rooms with mysterious packages half hidden in their arms!

Many families have found the joy that comes from sharing with others, especially at Christmas time. One family shares this joy with neighbors by giving a party for their children's friends. One year it is a Mothers and Daughters Tea, a lovely afternoon affair when all the little girls and their mothers are invited to a special open house. The house is decorated with attractive Christmas decorations in every room. The Christmas tree stands in splendor in the living room and a cheerful fire glows in the hearth. In the dining room a beautifully decorated table is laden with delicious food, graced by a silver tea service and a punch bowl. Teen-age cousins and sub-teen daughters assist with the serving. The sound of lovely Christmas music fills the air as the guests are made welcome by the Mother and her daughters acting as hostesses.

Another year, a Caroling Party is held, with families including parents, grandparents, and children all being invited to join in an evening of Christmas singing. The guests sit informally on the stairs, on the floor, and overflow into the hall, and, accompanied by a piano, they heartily sing all the well loved carols. Light refreshments are served at the end of the evening and everyone toasts the wassail cup before going out into the chilly night.

A Cookie Baking Party is another fun way to entertain. The children are invited as honored guests and helpers. They make simple sugar cookies and gingerbread men. They roll out, cut out, bake, and decorate to their hearts' content. Samples are tasted on the spot with chocolate milk or cider and each guest takes some cookies home as a treat.

Another version of family-neighborhood entertaining is the Sugar 'n Spice Party. Like the Cookie Bake, it is a cooperative affair, only the guests make candy instead of cookies. It can be an old-fashioned candy pull with taffy bubbling on the stove while guests play a game or sing some carols. Or it can be more elaborate with several kinds of candy made. The guests are given colorful aprons and told the recipes and ingredients to be used. Then they divide into groups, each group making a different kind of candy. The stove plus an electric saucepan or two provide adequate cooking surfaces. After the clean-up is good-naturedly finished, each guest takes home tangible evidence of a gay evening—a holly-sprigged box of candy.

There is no end to the various and delightful ways a family can "keep" Christmas.

Keeping alive the joy that comes from finding a filled stocking on Christmas morning, one family with grown children has everyone hang a stocking on the fireplace about the middle of December, with the solemn promise from all not to peek until Christmas morning. During the next week or so, knots and bumps of unusual shapes appear in the stocking as family members hide various gifts for each other from day to day.

Another family has a very special way of wishing all the children in the neighborhood a Merry Christmas. Each Christmas Eve the family makes the rounds of homes in the neighborhood and leaves a large, decorated, *personalized* gingerbread boy for each child. These gingerbread men are made with much expectancy and happiness several days before Christmas. They are decorated richly with raisin eyes and nose, gay buttons, and a frosting inscription of each child's name. A perky red ribbon bow is tied around the gingerbread neck. He is now ready to hang on a tree where arm by arm and leg by leg he will disappear. What joy this simple tradition brings to the givers and the recipients.

A "Bright Light" tour has proved to be an exciting holiday event in one family we know. Each year they travel to the nearest large city and spend an afternoon and evening on the town, featuring dinner at a restaurant and a leisurely tour of the shop window displays and brilliantly lighted Christmas decorations.

Another family makes a special event out of "read-aloud" sessions held in front of the fire on early December evenings. Father, Mother, and the older children take turns reading all or excerpts from some of the favorite Christmas stories and poems such as the "Bird's Christmas Carol," Edna Baker's beautiful "A Child is Born," Dickens'

Christmas Carol, "In Clean Hay," Longfellow's "The Three Kings," and the Christmas chapters from *Five Little Peppers* and *Little House in the Woods.* The evening is made festive with cocoa and cookies and closes with family prayers. Those magical bedtime sessions have a way of making Christmas seem the most wonderful thing that ever happened to the world—as indeed it is.

One family has a tradition of toy-mending each Christmas. To help their boys visualize that the joy of giving is enhanced by giving of oneself, each year their friends are invited to contribute broken but mendable toys to be repaired and repainted by this father and his three sons. Several weeks before Christmas their basement workshop is a busy place, with saw, hammer, and paint brushes being wielded with enthusiasm and earnestness. The rewards of this custom have been many. Not only have the boys learned how to use tools expertly, and known the satisfaction of reclaiming something of worth, but they have seen that love is increased through shared responsibilities, and they appreciate the closeness that comes with working together.

The Twelve Days of Christmas

One neighborhood has the custom of celebrating the Twelve Days of Christmas, a tradition that flourished in the Middle Ages. Their celebration started on Christmas day with a worship service for all the families. On each day thereafter, until Epiphany, a family activity is planned. It might be cookie baking one day, seeing a performance of "The Nutcracker" ballet the next. Other days feature a trip downtown to see the decorations in the store windows, a concert, and a sleigh ride. Each day brings some pleasant surprise and though the display of gifts on Christmas day is not as lavish as in other households, the children in the neighborhood look forward to each day with joy and fulfillment.

A family of teen-agers celebrates the end of the holidays with a Twelfth Night Party. At this time each year they lay aside small gifts —memo pads, homemade sweets, or handkerchiefs—and wrap them in leftover Christmas wrappings. These are put under the tree. In the evening, the children strip the tree of its ornaments and carefully pack them away for next year. Each one opens one of the little gifts and then the tree comes down. The greens are burned in the fireplace and all the Christmas candles are lighted and burned down to the last bit of wax.

A big pot of chili on the stove provides a hearty supper for everyone. Each one fills his own tray in the kitchen and then they gather around the fire to eat. A basket of rye bread, pickles, relishes, and milk or cocoa are handy on the coffee table. The remains of the Christmas fruitcake finishes their supper. The spicy scent of the burning greens and the warm glow of the red candles complete the setting. As the family sings its favorite carols for the last time the night outside is as beautiful and still as hope and faith.

In another home the children have a tree "farewell" in the form of breakfast under the tree the morning after New Year's when the tree is dismantled. This charming tradition started years ago when one of the young children couldn't bear the prospect of leaving the tree and going off to school. To soften the parting, the family carried breakfast into the living room, sat by the tree, and talked over the happy memories of Christmas. Each child took his favorite ornament from the tree and carefully put it away. Because it is usually on a school day, the "ceremony" is brief; juice, hot chocolate, crisp bacon, and English muffins are served on individual trays. After singing a final Christmas carol, each child is off to school. This fond farewell to the Christmas tree signifies all the suspense, excitement, and fun of Christmas and writes a happy *finis* to the holiday season.

5.

Something to Give

THE HAPPINESS THAT COMES WITH GIVING AND SHARING IS something children should learn early in life. And home is the best place to start learning. You might try a device as simple as the one used successfully by a family and called by them their "Treasure Chest." This chest consists of a cardboard box with a lid and is decorated and painted by the children. Inside the box is a veritable storehouse of treasures for children. All the items are inexpensive; most of them are from the dime store. Included are crayons, whistles, balloons, balls and jacks, candy treats, toy cars, and dolls. Many of the items would be discarded by some people but they are priceless treasures to a child, and the family can have fun looking for them and keeping the chest supplied.

The chest is brought out whenever a young guest visits the home. As a farewell gesture, each visiting child is allowed to choose something from the box to take as a keepsake. Imagine what joy this brings to the young visitor!

The always in-and-out neighborhood children are not included in this ritual regularly, but on special occasions surprises are shared with them, too.

One of the happiest families we know makes a practice of bringing joy to newcomers in their neighborhood by an expressive gesture of good will. Realizing how hectic moving and setting up housekeeping in a new home can be, this family has endeared itself to others by providing a welcome lunch or supper to people moving into their neighborhood. This simple meal, consisting of a hot casserole or a tureen of hearty soup, rolls, vegetable relishes or a fruit salad, cake or cookies, is a real lifesaver to a tired-out family still contemplating unmade beds, dishes to be unpacked, and household wares stacked all over the floor. Paper plates, napkins, cups, and silverware are furnished so that the cleaning-up is no problem.

This same family helps make moving out of the neighborhood easier too. They try to provide the last meal, especially if it's breakfast, so everything can be packed the night before with no last minute fussing about food, pots, and pans.

In a neighborhood containing families of three major faiths, one mother made great strides in creating understanding and love when she decided to invite the other neighborhood families to share in a party celebrating the family's next religious holiday. Invitations were sent out and families of all faiths attended. The house was decorated with holiday decorations and refreshments unique to that holiday were served.

The party was such a great success that the practice soon caught on. Other inter-faith parties were held and these helped all the families gain a better understanding of other customs and beliefs. This understanding increased the feeling of friendship in the neighborhood.

For summertime fun, one neighborhood has a round-the-block parade with the children decorating wagons, trikes, and bicycles for a colorful entourage. Simple floats are made by using a wagon for a base and putting a board across the wagon bed. Easy floats might include the following: Boxing ring: four post supports are fastened to the corners of the wagon with ropes on each side forming a "ring." "Boxers" sit on small stools, wearing boxing shorts and gloves. Indian float: a tepee made from a colorful rug or blanket is supported by a camera tripod. Sagebrush or evergreen trimmings are used as ground cover. A feather headband or an Indian costume is worn by the "Chiefs." Little Black Sambo: this story-book character wears a blue shirt, red jacket, and carries a green umbrella. A tiger costume adorns another child. A grass hut is made by covering a bushel fruit basket with a grass skirt. A tall palm tree is made by wrapping a cardboard mailing tube with brown crêpe paper and adding green crêpe paper leaves.

Three-generation parties can be lots of fun if everyone enters into the spirit of the occasion with the idea of contributing to the pleasure of the evening. We have found this experience most satisfying, and on numerous occasions we have invited entire families—grandparents, parents, and children—to spend an evening of fun with us. We frequently make a basketball game or movie the occasion to include the grandparents. Children need the association with older people to round out their lives and to appreciate the family relationship in its fullness. Being together with other members of the family helps bridge the gap between generations. As the guests pair off in partners, grandfather and a granddaughter, Mother and young son, Dad and grandmother, each gets a different type of association from the usual companionship. Deeper love and compatability, as well as hours spent in laughing together, are the dividends.

The Caroling Party on page 35 and the Mother and Daughters Tea on page 35 feature parties with two or more generations getting together for fun. These are carefully planned affairs and take some preparation, but the same results can be obtained by informal, even spur-of-the-moment parties. For example, if the fence needs painting, or the autumn leaves need raking, Tom Sawyer's old ruse still works like a charm! We invite families to share in the work with a promise of food and fun to follow.

One of the most fabulous ideas we've heard about for sharing family work and fun with others was the "crafteteria" party planned by an energetic and civic-minded family. The first "crafteteria" evening was held to make holiday favors for patients at a local hospital. The family invited several neighbors to join them to get the job done as quickly as possible. When the other families arrived, they found the play room set up with card tables covered with odds and ends of materials: felt, sequins, glue, pipe cleaners, pins, colored and plain paper, foil, pencils, poster paints, brushes, scissors, and staples. The hosts also had on display a number of suggestions and samples for decorative favors. The guests were instructed to use their own creative talents and imaginations to make anything they desired. They could keep what they made or donate it to the worthy project. At first, guests were hesitant about starting, but after one or two clever ideas developed, they gained confidence and worked eagerly. Soon a variety and quantity of original and delightful favors were ready for distribution at the hospital. Since this first successful evening a number of "crafteteria" parties have been held with various objectives. One was an evening spent making Christmas decorations. One was a toy repair night. Light refreshments are always served and someone usually plays the piano while the others sing as they work.

You may like to invite several other families to join you for dinner some evening and make it a cooperative affair with each family helping with part of the menu. A cook-out or picnic makes a delightful family get-together with other families included. Let the children help in the preparation. In the fall you and another family might like to try a nut gathering expedition, taking a picnic along. Or try taking a drive into the hills to see the brilliant display of autumn leaves, stopping for lunch along the way.

Another way to share with families is to invite them to a dessert party. They have their dinner at home and join you for dessert only. You may want to play a game or two, watch a good TV show or have an evening of home movies.

You can invite other families to share in a talent show, barbeque, an evening of music, a game night, or a candy-making session. It's not so important what you do, as it is that you *do* it. The important thing is to share pleasant hours and experiences with others, thereby encouraging your children to be hospitable and to feel at ease with others.

Write Me a Letter

It is possible to share happiness as well as news by writing letters to friends or relatives away from home. Everyone loves to receive mail, especially those who are in distant places and miss the close association of family and friends. Why don't you make it a project to share your family hours with others by writing to loved ones away from home? Set aside an hour when everyone in the family can add a paragraph or two to the letters and be sure to include all the news items, current anecdotes, and personal experiences of those at home. Even very small children can participate by "telling" a letter to an older person who writes it down in the child's exact words. These letters will be most welcome to the receivers and will shorten the distance that separates them from home. Many families have fun with round-robin letters, and if your family is scattered you might like this method of communication.

6.

The Family Meets at Meal Times

Very often mealtime is the only time throughout a busy day when all the members of the family get together. In some families even mealtime is chaotic. In others, it is the best looked-forward-to time of all, when the family can sit down and break bread together and share ideas, anecdotes, and the experiences of the day. In many homes the dinner hour is indeed the family hour. In fact, the activities of the family hour can often be combined with the dinner hour when an event such as a birthday, anniversary, or special achievement of some family member occurs.

One family uses mealtime for all kinds of celebrations. For example, whenever one mother and father go on a trip they leave a cake decorated with a message written in icing to be served to the children at dinnertime while they are away. Whenever a family member returns home from a trip, he is greeted with a welcome home party with all the trimmings. In this way the family avoids the letdown feeling that is often the aftermath of returning home from an exciting trip or visit. It takes such a little bit of extra effort. A few candles, flowers for a centerpiece, or some other decoration and, presto, they have a dinner party.

However, every meal can't be a party. In every family there is sure to come the time when meal planning must be a hurried-up affair.

Nearly every mother on occasion has arrived home from a shopping trip or a club meeting to find that the hour is later than she thought. Surely there is no time to prepare the meal planned early in the day. Some quick substitute is needed—and in a hurry. You might find one mother's solution helpful the next time this happens to you. Long ago she established the custom of having a "Heidi Supper" on such occasions. The menu consists, naturally, of warm milk, cheese, and freshly-baked bread. And how good it tastes when it is presented in such a wholesome and delightful way. This otherwise simple fare takes on new dimensions of acceptability when presented as the favorite meal of Heidi, Peter, and the Alm Uncle. It can't be used too often, of course, but it is a real lifesaver when an emergency arrives and you have a hungry family to feed in a matter of minutes. Why not try a "Heidi Supper" next time you're caught with little time to prepare a meal!

What a nice event it is when the whole family goes out to have dinner at their favorite dining place. It's a treat for mother and the children and can be a pleasant experience for all if the children have been taught proper table manners and know how to behave in public places. A little preparation beforehand will be helpful in avoiding unpleasant experiences.

Sometimes children get restless when dining out, especially if there is a long wait for the food to be served. One resourceful mother keeps her children entertained by providing each child with a few decorative seals and an envelope containing some long narrow strips of colored paper. Using the seals to hold the strips of paper, the children arrange gas-pipe effects by attaching the strips at various angles. Sometimes a simple crossword puzzle, brought from Mother's purse during the waiting time, diverts attention and makes the time go faster. Or a favorite guessing game can be played during an interim such as this.

Try Some Table Games

Some interesting table games with action are listed below. We don't exactly recommend them for restaurant meals. They are fun to play at home at the end of the meal.

Table symphony. After dinner, while everyone is sitting around the table, relaxed and in a happy mood, you might like to have a little music of your own making. To have a table symphony you need water goblets. Each goblet is filled with a different amount of water. Dampen the tips of your fingers, then run them lightly over the rim of the goblet in a circular motion. Continue rimming the goblet until a sound is heard. It will be on a definite pitch and each glass will have a different tone. You might try synchronizing the sounds!

Here is a fun test that is a good after-dinner entertainment. Give each player a copy and just have him follow instructions to the surprise ending. It's amazing how many brilliant and intelligent people fail this very simple test. This is also fun to play at a party. Teenagers and adults will both enjoy it.

TEST

Name:_____

CAN YOU FOLLOW WRITTEN INSTRUCTIONS?

Note: *This is a timed test. You will be allowed three minutes only.*

1. Read everything carefully before doing anything.
2. Write your last name in the upper right hand corner of this sheet.
3. Draw a circle around the word "name" in the second sentence.
4. Draw five small squares in the name space in the upper left hand corner of the sheet.
5. Make an "X" in each square.
6. Stand up and call out your first name when you read this sentence.
7. Print "yes" after the title at top of page.
8. Make an "X" in the lower left hand corner of this sheet.
9. Underline #7 sentence.
10. Multiply 70 by 61 on back of this sheet.
11. Call out "I have" if you have followed all directions carefully to this point.
12. Circle all even numbers.
13. Count from ten to one backwards in a normal voice.
14. Draw a square around each number that is spelled out on this sheet.
15. Now that you have finished reading everything carefully, follow the directions in sentence two *only*.

Many children eat their noon meal at school each day and don't have the midday contact with mother and home. This makes a long day from early morning until mid-afternoon, especially for the newly-turned school-age child. But you can still keep that little touch of love and thoughtfulness that means "home" by tucking small treats and messages into each lunchbox you pack. This is a wonderful way to keep up morale especially when it has been a bad day.

If your child is very young, try folding simple notes or funny pictures into his napkin. As he gets older, add cartoons or notes such as "Let's go for a walk after school," or "This is the day to get those new shoes. Hurry home!" "Here's a nickel to spend at Ernie's," or "The extra cupcake is for that A in arithmetic!" Children look forward to the little surprises and it takes the monotony out of eating lunch every day at school. At holiday time gaily decorated napkins of the season or a small favor does the trick. Extra goodies to share with best friends or a tiny gift are special treats for birthdays. On busy days just a "Hi" or "I love you" printed across the napkin will convey the message of affection between home and child. Try it with your children, or even with Dad if he carries a lunch to work. It's a great morale booster!

Drive-Inn Picnics

Do you hesitate to take your children out to eat because of the expense? If you do, you might compromise the way one family does. They celebrate occasionally by going to the drive-in movie and taking supper with them. A simple picnic lunch is the bill of fare and individually wrapped servings make it easy to control spills and clutter. The supper is arranged on individual TV dinner trays, and each tray is wrapped in a bandana napkin. Each person then eats as he views the movie. When finished, he wraps the tray up in the bandana again and takes care of the scraps when he returns home. The picnic supper makes it possible to go to the show and see the movie before the hour gets late and the children get too sleepy. These "Drive-Inn" Picnics are favorites with everyone in the family.

And speaking of picnics, after a series of "spur-of-the-moment" picnics in which we invariably arrived at the spot only to find we'd forgotten the matches, the salt, or the paper napkins, we decided to get organized. We found a good-sized square suitcase in an army surplus store. It had been used as a camera case during the war. We lined it with red and white checkered plastic and sectioned it off with pieces of thin plywood. The lid was fitted with elastic holders to keep plates and silverware in their proper places. Half-inch elastic was fastened with little bolts and nuts to make it secure. A list of the contents was pasted in the lid for quick checking. It includes the following: matches; newspapers; paper napkins; tablecloth; paper towels; wax paper bags; plastic containers for salads, sandwiches, and vegetables; aluminum foil; salt and pepper; plastic plates, cups, knives, forks, and spoons; serving spoons; paring knives; bread knife; can opener; bottle opener; bottle of cocoa and sugar mix; powdered milk; long-handled fork; and pot holders.

7.

Manners Are
the Measure of Love

Though few of us believe that knighthood is in flower, still it's a rare day that goes by without affording an opportunity for each of us to prove his gallantry. Though the cape-in-the-mud routine has gone out of style, good manners and courtesy are still important to all of us.

We are firmly convinced that good manners are essential even in our present day informality, and we think children should be taught correct social behavior in the home. Since we are convinced that social skills are not instinctive but must be learned, we try to allow time in our family night schedule to *practice* good manners. We realize, of course, that a good example is very important but we don't think a good example is enough. Some skills develop slowly with consistent practice, and we believe good manners and social graces are such skills. Just as most children have to practice the piano diligently to become skillful, so we think most children must practice standing when an older person enters the room, must practice opening and closing the doors quietly, must practice greeting guests, and so on through all the long list of acceptable manners that help smooth our relationships with other people.

Genuine Concern for Others

Of course, genuine courtesy goes beyond mechanical politeness, which is often cold and perfunctory. Real courtesy is warm and shows itself in genuine concern for others' comfort and well-being. Good manners are nothing more than thinking of others and being considerate of them.

Everyone recognizes the fact that there are certain homes where charm and warmth are found in more abundance than in others. Naturally, the fortunate child of such a household will be imbued with the spirit of friendliness and will be more apt to gain self-confidence in how to greet guests, how to put a stranger at ease, and how to help others overcome self-consciousness.

Every wallflower longs for popularity. But many parents don't realize that a little extra effort on their part can help their teen-age son or daughter achieve social ease. If early training in good manners is established as a natural part of the home, the average boy or girl can bypass many of the difficulties of adolescence. Ask any teen-ager what the greatest social difficulties are and he will answer: lack of confidence in making and acknowledging introductions, inability to open or maintain a conversation, self-consciousness when meeting strangers. Every one of these problems should be met and conquered in childhood. Habits of good grooming and proper dress should also be established early in life.

One family whose children are exceptionally well-mannered, made it a habit over the years to practice one social grace each week. In time, this effort has been rewarded handsomely. Some of the subjects they have practiced include: what to do when calling on others, how to behave in public places, how to behave in church, being kind to those less fortunate, how to show appreciation to others by writing thank you notes or telephoning to express thanks, being considerate of other people's feelings, and sincerely apologizing when you happen to offend someone.

Good manners include respecting other people's wishes for privacy. This is especially important during the teen-age years. One mother showed respect and understanding for her daughter's newly developed wish for privacy by giving her a little brass knocker for the door of her room. The knocker reminded other family members to "mind their manners," and gave the daughter a feeling of being recognized as a young adult.

Here are some practical and everyday manners that would be good to talk about during the family hour.

1. Excuse yourself when you leave a room.
2. Do favors cheerfully.
3. Speak quietly.
4. Return things you borrow.
5. Knock before entering someone's room.
6. Keep promises you have made.
7. Not open or read another's mail.
8. Remain standing until older people are seated.
9. Say a cheerful "good morning" and "good night."
10. Not open another's bureau drawers without permission.
11. Not take longer than necessary in the bathroom.
12. Clean the basin and tub after using.
13. Not interrupt when others are speaking.
14. Talk quietly when riding in a bus or car.
15. Not be boisterous or loud in public places.
16. Not write on public property.
17. Not push or crowd when standing in line.
18. Come to the table clean and neat and in a happy mood.
19. Talk of interesting and pleasant things.
20. Use good table manners so that eating is a pleasant experience.

Good Manners and Good Sportsmanship Go Together

Good sportsmanship is closely related to good manners and, like good manners, is based on consideration and respect for others. What is good sportsmanship, and why is it desirable in developing character? Your children might enjoy taking the following quiz and discussing the questions involved. Answer each question "yes" or "no" or "sometimes."

HOW DO YOU RATE IN SPORTSMANSHIP?

1. Do you like to play almost every kind of game?
2. Are you always willing to play games that others want to play?
3. Do you always obey the rules of the game?
4. Are you always fair in taking your turn?
5. Do you accept the decision of the umpire or of the group?

6. Can you win without boasting about it?
7. Can you lose without grumbling or making excuses?
8. Do you keep your temper when you and others make mistakes?
9. Do you believe in giving every person the opportunity to play?
10. Do you listen carefully to instructions and follow directions?
11. Are you courteous to those who play with you?
12. Do you share your play equipment and other possessions?

If you have ten "yes" answers, you are a good sport. If you have more than four questions answered "sometimes," you need to improve. If you have more than four "no" answers, you are probably a poor sport.

Good Manners in Speech

Good manners also carry over into habits of speech. Children should be taught very early in life the axiom:

> *Hearts, like doors, will open with ease*
> *To very, very little keys.*
> *And don't forget that two of these*
> *Are "Thank you, Sir," and "If you please."*

Small children often pick up bad words they hear, and older children often say these words to show off or sound "tough." It might be worth your time to discuss the effects of this kind of language and explain that most people who use such words often do so because they are not well enough educated to express themselves eloquently without swear words; that educated people have a good command of words so they can say what they want to explicitly and interestingly. You might want to acquaint your children with "Roget's Thesaurus" and have them learn to use it when struggling for a word in speaking or when writing.

A good rule to practice in conversation at home is that anyone caught interrupting or talking when another is talking must pay a forfeit.

So you see, good manners—in word or in gesture—can be practiced everyday, countless times a day—try counting the ways in which good manners are contributing to happiness in *your* family life.

8.

Looking into Things

CHILDREN ARE BORN LOVING THE BEAUTIFUL. TO CHILdren, a dandelion, a raindrop, a star is beautiful and mysterious. They want to touch and feel everything. And as parents, we must cultivate their love of beauty and guide its course. Otherwise, we might dull their natural appreciation for what is beautiful in life. Our children are going to grow up to be adults and we don't want them to be adults who trample on the beauties of nature, who deface and litter our national parks and highways. No, we must help them love and appreciate beauty for its own sake.

Our living habits and environment have undergone some drastic changes in the last generation. With fewer and fewer people living on farms or in the country, it is sometimes difficult to provide a natural background for our children to learn about the beauties of nature.

For children who do not live on a farm with ponies, horses, and other animals, it is sometimes easy to overlook the possibilities of companionship with animals. But even in a city apartment, experiences with living creatures can be had. True, you won't be able to stable a pony or raise rabbits, but you can have small pets that will help the child learn to care about the world around him—the greater world in which he lives. Guppies, parakeets, turtles, perhaps a kitten or a puppy can be housed in a city apartment. An aquarium is a world of its own. Goldfish and other exotic fish require little space and are fascinating to watch. Even a garden is possible, especially if it is an exquisite miniature garden such as those the Japanese are so skilled in creating.

For a child who loves growing things, a herb garden can be a fine hobby and is a good substitute for an outdoor garden where space is limited. A plastic tray, herb seeds, soil, vermiculite, and a guide book such as *The Adventure Book of Growing Plants* by Francis M. Mineo (Capitol) will start a child out on an adventure in the wonders of nature.

The normal, natural relationship between life and death can most easily be taught by the association of living things. Many children now grow to adulthood learning about life and death only through the sordid, meaningless "accidents" of death as pictured in newspapers, movies, and on TV. Respect for the natural cycle of life and death and for the sacredness of living things can be beautifully emphasized as children are taught to handle pets with gentleness and care. Any tendency to cruelty should not be allowed to develop.

Any family can undertake a marvelous study of the natural world right in its own back yard or nearby park. In the insect and nature worlds can be found the most fundamental values of growth, maturity, and death. The life cycle can be followed in the miniature world of a spider or an ant. By observing with reverence the life of God's other living creatures, children learn more about understanding their own role in the world. The wonderful world of birds and butterflies, of fireflies and frogs can awaken a child's appreciation of himself. It can help deepen the understanding of himself and his surroundings.

In his own back yard a child can find close-at-hand knowledge about creatures that will enhance and enlarge his whole scope of appreciation for the seasons—spring, summer, fall, and winter. By watching the activities of spiders spinning webs, a caterpillar spinning a cocoon, or a tadpole emerging as a frog, a child can develop a sustaining interest in life's many miraculous changes. The transformation of a tadpole is exciting because a child can see the changes taking place each day. And the metamorphosis of a butterfly is really breathtaking. The change from a crawling, creeping caterpillar to a beautiful fragile butterfly is so completely amazing! Children can closely watch the process by collecting caterpillars and keeping them in small wooden boxes while they spin their cocoons.

Let's Collect Things

As children become aware of the changes and beauties in the world around them, it is second nature to want to collect the evidence of these beauties. The child's inclination to collect all manner of objects often becomes a lifelong pursuit with many people. Little boys collect rocks, sticks, bugs, and all manner of wondrous stuff. Little girls collect paper dolls and miniature dishes; teens collect movie-star pictures, sports cards, records, and photographs. Almost everyone collects something.

Today, more than ever before, Mother, Dad, and the children are finding the pleasure of enjoying collections together. One of the best time-tested family hobbies is that of *stamp collecting*. It appeals to both children and adults because it can be enjoyed in various degrees, depending on the years and maturity of the individual. Children can be avid collectors without considering the more serious pursuits that delight the adult collector who may be more exacting and discriminating. Stamp collecting has many facets, depending upon the interest of the individual. If Dad likes cars, he might find pleasure in collecting stamps featuring automobiles. Mother might like to collect stamps from all over the world honoring flowers or children. Boys may collect stamps commemorating sports, boats, transportation, explorers or famous people. Almost every subject has been honored by stamps from many countries.

Coin collecting has the same advantages as stamp collecting. It takes up little space. It can lead to an interest in related subjects such as history or cultures of other countries. Coin collecting can teach young people or adults as much about money as a banker knows! Many hobby shops and five and dime stores carry coin folders which keep coins classified and in good shape.

Rock collecting as a family hobby will bring many hours of outdoor fun and it will also help increase your knowledge of plants, animals, birds, geography, and history. There are some excellent inexpensive source books that will be helpful to you in the pursuit of this hobby, including *How to Know Rocks and Minerals* ($1.00), a Signet Key Book by Richard M. Picol; *Reptiles and Amphibians* ($1.00), a Golden Nature Guide; *Rocks and Minerals* ($1.00) and *Seashores* ($1.00) are published by the Golden Nature Guide series.

Collecting rocks and studying the geology of the earth's surface can become an open door to the drama of the earth's history. Many wonderful and productive hours can be spent by the family in exploring areas around the home. As you learn to identify rocks and minerals, you will gain an appreciation of the many events that have happened in the earth's history. A minimum of equipment is needed. A sturdy field bag for holding specimens, a geologist's hammer and chisel, a magnifying glass, a note book, and a field guide will be useful. Old quarries, rock pits, and excavations will all provide interesting specimens.

This is an activity that the whole family can share. As you explore the areas around your home and visit mountains, deserts, and seashores in search of interesting rocks, you will become aware of many other interesting facts about the country in which you live. You may even enjoy the thrill of finding early Indian artifacts or mounds among your explorations.

If you and your children love the sea, if you feel the primordial influence of it, then *shell collecting* will help you probe the world where the land and the waters meet. Here again, if your hobby is going to be rewarding, you will want to study a guide book to help you identify and classify your shells. Simon & Schuster publishes *Seashores* by Zim and Ingle, an excellent book of source material. Reference sets such as the *World Book* will also help you with your study of shells.

If you have a collection of sea shells, you will find a new and delightful use for them if you combine your shell collection with an interest in gardening. Shell gardens are a new version of an old idea and are really dish gardens with spaghnum moss used in place of soil. The delicate and fragile beauty of shells makes an extraordinary setting for miniature plants. You will want to use small plants for your shell gardens, such as succulents, English ivy, maidenhair fern, strawberry begonia, chlorophytum, syngonium, and dwarf jade. In repotting the plants, be careful that the roots are not injured. Carefully tease and squeeze the soil from the roots and rewrap the roots in moist spaghnum moss of the proper size and shape for inserting into the shell. These miniature shell gardens will last for months with proper care, and they make a beautiful and unusual gift for a shut-in.

Since we have emphasized the joy of understanding the earth beneath us and the sea around us, we must not overlook the wonders of the sky above us.

Since the manned space flights, the interest in astronomy and star gazing has increased immensely. It's fascinating to track the satellites in orbit and, if you have a rudimentary knowledge of the universe, sky-watching can be fun for the whole family. To make the family interest more knowledgable, all you need is a book on astronomy such as *The Golden Book of Astronomy* (Golden Press). This book has a constellation chart to guide your star-gazing.

In good weather, on a clear night, spend an hour with the family, all lying down on a blanket, gazing at the stars. A simple map, book, or pamphlet about the stars will be helpful, such as *Star Legends* (Clark Wissler) published by the American Museum of Natural History. A telescope will add much to your study of the skies. Many models are available in every budget range.

Displaying Collections

If your family has an interesting collection of stamps, shells, or travel pennants, then you may be inspired to display them in some attractive way. Stamps, coins, or rocks can be artistically framed and displayed on walls. Shells, minerals, bird nests, beehives, and other natural objects can be displayed on shelves or in cases. Collections of drawings by budding artists in the family, made from kindergarten days on, can be a real decorative feature if framed and arranged on a wall in a colorful display. Photographs, until recently relegated to drawers, are now coming into their own again. You might like to display your collection in attractive groups.

Handicrafts open up another wide field of hobbies for the family to enjoy. For example, one entire family became interested in clay modeling after one of the children joined a sculpture class. At a small cost, they built a kiln of firebricks in their back yard and wired it for electricity. They made all kinds of articles. The older children make their own plastic molds and pour their clay into them to create lovely articles of beauty and usefulness. The younger children press designs into the clay with almost anything, a match stick, a fork, or a leaf. The hobby is a very satisfying one for the family, and their home and friends benefit from it.

Art

A home-study course in art can be lots of fun for the family. You may want to begin with the Metropolitan Museum Art Seminar series which provides rich and colorful background material for the lay art student. The beautiful reproductions of famous paintings and the discussions contained in each of the twelve portfolios are a priceless addition to a home interested in cultural pursuits.

If your family enjoys painting and has a knack for it, why don't you try taking an art course together at the local university or adult education service? Many communities have artists groups who offer basic courses in painting and it may be that your family would benefit from such instruction. "Sunday painters" have wonderful times experimenting with paint and canvas.

Arts

If you can't afford private instruction in some of the fields in which you would like to expand your knowledge, and even if you can afford them, you will find instructional records which will be a helpful aid to your study program. The field of "How-to" records is increasing everyday and already a wide range of subjects is available. Records that teach will open up a whole wide world to families interested in acquiring new skills. You can learn Russian, Morse code, contract bridge, banjo playing, the cha-cha, or touch typing. You can learn languages, music, drama, games, and skills of many kinds. You can even learn how to make money from records prepared by New York Stock Exchange experts! Of course, you don't get out of it any more than you put into it. You have to supply the willingness to work and learn.

In the army, new recruits are given indoctrination or orientation courses. In your own family, this technique will prove helpful when you are planning a trip or a new adventure in family living. A short briefing can do wonders for helping parents and children appreciate what is to come, whether it be a trip to the north woods, a trip to a concert, or a holiday celebration. Learning the origin and background of any subject will help you to appreciate and enjoy that subject more. One family calls their family hour program just that—orientation night. Because whatever is in the offing, whether it be a new movie, a book, a sightseeing tour, a trip to Timpanogos Cave, or an art exhibit, they do a little preliminary research with reference books and encyclopedias. A wonderful store of information and appreciation for events and places has been the result of these planning sessions.

Family History

Try writing a family history for your children, your children's children, and their children. It's rewarding to know about what great-great-grandfather did as he crossed the plains in a covered wagon in 1852. It's fascinating to hear about a forefather who joined the freedom forces in General Washington's army in 1776. It gives each child a sense of pride in his heritage to know that some adventurous ancestor left his homeland to venture forth to a new and undeveloped country, meeting hardships and privations with fortitude and courage. On family nights, we retell some of these exciting experiences, and we record current ones that are happening now to our children and in time will be of interest to their children and grandchildren. The early explorations into outer space will be as interesting to our grandchildren as the exploration of the West, written by our grandparents, are to us!

Special Events

When someone in the family achieves recognition or honor, a special citation is awarded him on family night. Perhaps John is elected as a school officer, David achieves a new rank in Scouting, Mom becomes a PTA officer, Dad is appointed a club or community service chairman, or Carol makes the honor roll—then it's time for a brief ceremony to pay honor to the one meriting recognition. We do this for two reasons: first, we want them to know we are all proud of them, and second, we want them to know that as a family we are behind them and will support them wholeheartedly in their new position of responsibility. Sometimes a small gift accompanies the brief ceremony. It is given with love, affection, and pride in their accomplishments.

9.

The Enjoyment of Books
and Story-Telling

It's a far cry from Abraham Lincoln sprawled in front of a fireplace with a book he had walked miles to borrow, to the present-day youngster sprawled in front of a TV set absorbing mediocrity. In the past, even among rather moderately well-to-do people, a man's library was a source of great pride. Contrast this with the rather startling survey made today showing that in 12,000 new homes being built in a flourishing suburb, not a book shelf of any kind was designed! This doesn't refer to just book shelves, this refers to *any* shelves for reading material of *any* kind. In fact, in the last ten years, only 12 per cent of the homes built have any shelves for reading materials. And this has been in a period of unprecedented prosperity and leisure time! Surely it's time for a "wake up and read" campaign.

The sum total of our human knowledge is contained in books. Our whole civilization is based on books. Without the printed word we would still be in darkness. As Phyllis McGinley, Pulitzer Prize winner, says:

"Since the invention of the printed word, people have been seduced by the powers of the printed word. They have been converted to religion, inspired to patriotism, lured into sin and lured into salvation. It was with a book that Martin Luther sparked the Reformation, by a book that St. Ignatius was won from the life of a Basque cavalier to that of God's soldier. Not all the tea dumped into Boston harbor was as influential in bringing about the American Revolution as was Thomas Paine, busy with his tracts. Soviet Russia was bred in the brain of Karl Marx, scribbling away at *Das Kapital* in the British Museum. St. Augustine came to Christianity by way of a book. We are all swayed, whether we know it or not, by what we read in a book."

Childhood is the time to begin to read books and to build storehouses of memory. It is a time for building castles, for reading fabulous adventures, for hobnobbing with giants in fact and fancy. Then the magic of that special place, or person, or event cannot so easily slip away in the years to come. Children need heroes. They need to know about Lancelot, Don Quixote, Dr. Thomas Dooley, Nathan Hale, Robert Frost, and Charles Lindbergh. They need to know about the past so they can understand the present and comprehend the future. And they cannot know the past unless they read about it in history, biography, philosophy, fiction, or poetry. As Mr. Justice Cardoza expressed: "You must study the wisdom of the past, for in a wilderness of conflicting counsels a trail has there been blazed. You will study the life of mankind, for this is the life you must order, and to order with wisdom, must know. You will study the precept of justice, for these are the truths that through you will come to their hour of triumph!"

Try Reading Aloud

Reading aloud has long been a favorite pastime for parents as well as children, especially those parents who are discriminating and desirous of giving their children the best introduction to the world of books. Even long after the child can read for himself, there is a magical relationship in a mother or father gathering the children around for this old-fashioned bedtime ritual. Recent emphasis has been given to this custom with the introduction of the Westinghouse series "Reading Out Loud " This TV program features famous Americans reading their favorite poems and stories to children.

Many parents wish to help their children to form good reading habits at an early age but are handicapped by a lack of knowledge about books. Experts believe that the best way to encourage children is for adults to be enthusiastic about their own enjoyment of books, and to expose children to good books without coercion. Here again, many parents are not informed enough to select good books without some assistance. A list of helpful books for parents seeking guidance for their children's reading follows:

Growing Up With Books—35¢—Bowker Co., 62 W. 45th St., New York 36, New York

Growing Up With Science Books—35¢—Bowker Co., 62 W. 45th St., New York 36, New York

Books, Young People and Reading Guidance—Hanna & McCallister. Harper

Children's Books Too Good to Miss—Arbuthenot, Clark, Horrocks and Lord. Western Reserve University Press (paperbound) $1.25

Annual "Notable Children's Books," Children's Service Division, American Library Association

Annual "Interesting Adult Books for Young People,' American Library Association

Parents' Guide to Children's Reading—Nancy Larrick. Pocket Books—35¢

Weekly Readers Children's Book Club, Education Center, Columbus 16, Ohio

Seven Stories High—Anne Carroll Moore (Supt. of Work With Children, New York Public Library). F. E. Compton Co., 100 N. Dearborn, Chicago 10, Ill.

Add Depth and Lilt With Poetry

John Ciardi, one of our best known poets, believes that a familiarity with poetry is essential to the truly educated man because poems are one of the means by which we achieve contact with the great minds that mold our culture. Answering a pharmacology student who believed that reading *Hamlet* was a waste of time, Mr. Ciardi said, "What will you do with the hours of your life left over from work and sleep? Let's say you will go home from work to your family. What sort of family are you raising? Will your children ever be exposed to a reasonably penetrating idea? Will you be presiding over a family that maintains some basic contact with the great continuity of democratic intellect? Or will your family life be strictly penny-ante and beer-on-ice? Will there be a book in the house? Will there be a painting a reasonably sensitive man can look at without shuddering? Will your family be able to speak English and to talk about an idea? Will the kids ever get to hear Bach?" Mr. Ciardi feels that if a person has no time for Shakespeare, for the enjoyment of the fine arts, for the story of man's development and history, then that person is on his way to being a "new species of mechanized savage—a push-button Neanderthal."

Children love poetry. They respond naturally to the rhythm of verse, and their sense of humor is well-keyed to the light verse of A. A. Milne, Dr. Seuss, Ogden Nash, Phyllis McGinley, Laura Richards, Rachel Field, Rose Fyleman and many others.

Whether children grow up liking poetry or not depends on how they are introduced to it and how well they have read poetry aloud and enjoyed happy experiences with it. The magic of poetry can fill even the most unimaginative child with a source of delight. When they have read a poem they have a sense of identification with its creator, and share with him for a moment that feeling of discovery he must have felt when he created the poem.

Poetry reading, either aloud by you and your family or on recordings, is coming back into vogue and will provide many hours of pleasure to the sensitive listener. The nonsense of Edward Lear, the rat-atat-tat of Edith Sitwell, the sound for its own sake of Gertrude Stein, the majestic phrases of Shakespeare were composed as much for the ear as for the mind and heart. Poetry, like music, is a vehicle for patterns of rhythm and sound, so its meaning comes alive when it is read aloud.

Choose a collection of poems from your favorite volumes and gather the family to share this reading experience. Try to read with meaning and inflection so that understanding and enjoyment will be increased.

Most people, especially children, enjoy poetry when it is used to evoke a rhythmic response. A *Pocketful of Poems* (Harper) by Marie Louise Allen is full of delightful poems to read aloud, including "Mitten Song," "Zipper Suit," and "Winter Wear." "Away We Go" by Eleanor Dennis is a good poem to march to, and Elinor Wylie's "Velvet Shoes" will make you want to tiptoe. "Feet" by Dorothy Aldis is lots of fun, as is her "Hiding." "Let's Pretend" by Jones

Tippett and "Quiet Please" by Emily Hilsabeck are fun to dramatize. "Houses" and "Moon Faces" by Aileen Fisher will inspire all the family to try illustrating and drawing.

A. A. Milne with his "Measles, Teazles and Sneazles" and his present day counterpart, Dr. Seuss, are never-ending sources of delight to children. Every home should have a copy of Milne's *When We Were Very Young* and *Now We Are Six* or Dr. Seuss' *I Visit the Zoo* and *The Cat in the Hat*.

To each new generation of children, Mother Goose rhymes are an endless source of pleasure. Children can swing along, trot, hop, skip, and gallop to them as they would to music. It's lots of fun to dramatize them too. Every home should have an excellent copy of Mother Goose with illustrations. Marguerite de Angeli's *Mother Goose* is one of our favorites.

While nothing takes the place of reading aloud yourselves, a wonderful collection of records featuring distinguished poets and great actors is now available. It is quite exciting to hear famous poets reading their own works. Robert Frost, T. S. Eliot, Ogden Nash, Carl Sandburg, and other great poets have recorded their own interpretations of their poems. Other famous poets, long dead, are brought to life by great artists such as Judith Anderson, Sir Ralph Richardson, Katherine Cornell, Sir John Gielgud, and others. Many famous actors have now recorded poems for children to hear, including artists such as Helen Hayes, Raymond Massey, Beatrice Lillie and Cyril Ritchard. Some of these records have an accompanying text but for those which do not, you will want to find the verses in printed form and follow with the eye as well as the ear.

A full listing of such records available can be found in the catalogues of your local record shop.

Tell Me A Story

Storytelling is so closely akin to reading that any family that enjoys the first should be an advocate of the second. It's most unfortunate that the ancient art of storytelling is fast being lost. This is true in large measure in all kinds of homes. With the advent of TV, with the craze for recreation, the joys and delights of reading and storytelling are being smothered. But it needn't be so. Wherever there is a father, mother, grandparent, brother, or sister who has discovered for himself the fun and pleasure to be derived from good stories, then there is a potential storyteller. Ruth Sawyer, one of the most famous storytellers, says that everyone is a potential storyteller. Nearly everyone, she says, has been telling stories since he learned to talk and everyone has a racial heritage passed on by traditional storytellers.

Just as in any art, certain skills are necessary. A pleasing voice, an adequate vocabulary, a certain amount of skill in using words are essential for a good storyteller, for words are to a storyteller what notes are to a musician and colors are to the artist. Families can use word games such as Scrabble or Anagrams to help build vocabularies that will make expression more fluent and increase the storyteller's confidence in his own ability to use words.

It is also important to understand a little about what makes a good story. Nearly all the familiar nursery tales, folk and fairy tales, stories of mythology and legends, make good stories for retelling. They have action, a simple plot, and an appropriate climax. A good story should have emotional appeal such as humor, courage, compassion, or love.

The timing of a story is just as important as selection of the story. Just as a symphony is not all played at the same tempo nor a dance danced to the same rhythm, so the tempo of a story should vary. The timing should be slow and leisurely when necessary and hurried when the action quickens. Pauses should be used for emphasis.

Sometimes it is interesting and entertaining to tell a story and record it on a tape or wire recorder. As the story unfolds, the sound effects of various animals, the weather, or other audible actions may be recorded. All the family will enjoy playing back the tape and listening to the story. For very young children, stories can be recorded with catchy ad-lib remarks or sounds to indicate the end of a page. As the pre-schooler listens to the record, he can follow the illustrations in the story book by listening for the signals to turn the page.

Storytelling can also be enhanced by using visual aids to highlight the characters and incidents in the story. Simple stories and poems can be illustrated in the easiest way with a few cut-outs or silhouettes that any child or adult can make. For example, just think of what fun and yet how simple it would be to illustrate on a flannel board the nursery rhyme:

> *It rained on Ann,*
> *It rained on Fran,*

> *It rained on Arabella,*
> *But it did not rain on Mary Jane,*
> *She had a big umbrella!*

Any child would have a good time cutting out the little girls from a magazine or coloring book, pasting a piece of flannel to the back of each, and adding a big paper umbrella to the scene.

Complex stories can be well told even by a beginner if they are good stories. The best guide for this is to choose stories by reputable authors. A source list follows:

The Art of Story Telling, Marie Shedlock (Dover)

The Way of the Storyteller, Ruth Sawyer (Viking)

How to Tell Stories to Children, Sara Cove Bryant (Houghton)

Family Reading Festival (Prentice-Hall)

Tales from Grimm, and *More Tales from Grimm*, translated and illustrated by Wanda Gag (Coward-McCann)

French Fairy Tales by Charles Perrault, retold by Louis Untermeyer (Didier)

East O'the Sun and West O'the Moon, Gudrun Thorne-Thompson (Row)

English Fairy Tales, Joseph Jacobs (Putnam)

Fairy Tales by Hans Christian Andersen (Coward-McCann)

Told Again, Walter de la Mare (Knopf)

Just So Stories, R. Kipling (Doubleday)

Wonder Clock, Howard Pyle (Scribner)

Rootabaga Stories, Carl Sandburg (Harcourt)

Jack Tales, Richard Chase (Houghton)

Favorite Uncle Remus, Joel Chandler Harris (Houghton)

Boy Who Could Do Anything and other Mexican Folk Tales, Anita Brenner (W. R. Scott)

Tales from Silver Lands, Charles J. Finger (Doubleday)

Beyond the Clapping Mountains, Charles Gillham (Macmillan)

Picture Tales from the Russian, Valery Carrick (Lippincott)

Czechoslovak Fairy Tales, Parker Fillmore (Harcourt)

Three Golden Oranges and other Spanish Folk Tales, Boggs and Davis (Longmans)

Well o'the World's End, Seumas MacManus (Devin-Adair)

Cow-Tail Switches and other West African Stories, Courlander and Herzog (Holt)

Once the Hodja, Alice Kelsey (Longmans)

Martin Pippin in the Daisy Field, Eleanor Farjeon (Lippincott)
Long Christmas, Ruth Sawyer (Viking)
Big Music, Mary Blecker (Viking)
Tales of Laughter, Kate Douglas Wiggin and Nora Smith (Doubleday)
Childcraft, Field Enterprises.

Many families have had "make believe" story characters who over the years have become so enmeshed in the children's lives that they are almost part of the family. Everyone in our family knows that when we talk about "Billy Johnson" we're talking about a pioneer boy who had many fabulous adventures crossing the plains and homesteading in the West with the early settlers. In our house, Billy is the favorite bedtime story character. His various escapades and harrowing escapes have endeared him to all the children. They feel a real kinship toward him since they identify themselves with his narrow brush with a rattlesnake, or his heroic efforts to get help when Indians attacked his homestead. Many delightful hours have been spent spinning out tales that show how this young boy survived in early pioneer days by using his wits, his courage, and his faith in God.

As part of any well ordered reading program children should be encouraged to work at building their vocabulary. Wide reading is the best aid in this, and the following techniques will help you:

1. Set up a goal of at least one serious book each month.
2. When you read, have a dictionary on hand and look up words.
3. Get acquainted with how the word is used and how it is pronounced. People sometimes try to be impressive by using big words and often use them incorrectly.

Also try vocabulary building by working crossword puzzles and then reading the dictionary. Not only a greater possible income, but also greater insight and confidence in yourself will result.

Vocabulary building and conversation training can both be complemented by family night programs that emphasize these skills. Many games that call for speaking abilities are fun to play. One of our favorites is the "Conversation Ball," made from various lengths of yarn, from two or three inches to several yards, all rolled together into a ball. The object of the game is to pass the ball around among the players, each one unwinding the yarn as he talks. He must continue talking as long as his piece of yarn lasts. When he comes to the end of his yarn, he passes the ball on to the next player. The player will only get to say a few words if the yarn is a short piece; if it is long, he can tell a longer incident. The game continues around the group until the yarn ball is all unwound.

Another vocabulary building game is "Stretching Words." The object is to start with a short word and then add a letter at a time to make another word, then add another letter to make another word, and so on until no more letters can be added. Give points to each person for each letter added to form a word. Some examples are: Ran, rain, train, trains, strains; or Ed, red, Fred, etc. "Ghosts" is a variation of this game where the player starts out with a letter and the next player tries to add another letter that will end in a word so the other players cannot add additional letters to form other words. As each word is finished, start with another letter.

If your family is reluctant to read, or not in the habit of reading, perhaps you could increase their interest in books by taking them to visit your local library. The library represents the wide, wide world in your community and on its shelves can be found all the adventures of life, adventures of thought as well as of action. From this beginning you might start building your own home library of books by giving well-chosen books as gifts for birthdays, Christmas, and other occasions.

Or if you are a reading family and have books that have become worn with age and repeated reading, perhaps you could spend a family hour together and hold a "Book Repair Night." Gather up all the books in the house that have loose pages and covers. Also have on hand glue or paste, staples, binding material such as leatherette or plastic, masking tape, Scotch or library tape, and scissors. Then you are all set for a book repair night and can have a very constructive hour getting your books back into a sturdy condition. Perhaps this would also be a good time to label all your books so they can be identified when borrowed or lost. A catalogue file of your books would be valuable to have. A simple classification system could be worked out for indexing your books in an orderly card file system.

10.

The Magic of Puppetry

Puppets are playthings—and much, much more. They help a child to be creative and imaginative, to experience the satisfaction of dramatizing a story, and to deeply appreciate the rich heritage of children's literature. The child is fortunate indeed who receives the rapt attention of his parents and family as his puppets dramatize a favorite story. Something really fine happens to the child —and to the spectators. All are bound closer together in mutual appreciation.

The best puppets for children are those they make for themselves. The FUN will be the children's most important objective—but the adults will also applaud the by-products of this activity: the manual abilities developed in the process, the growing self-reliance of the child as he moves away from the necessity of having his entertainment provided him, the satisfaction of applying creative imagination to making something that is useful and fun, and the confidence that comes with all these experiences.

Puppets can be used to illustrate any favorite story from children's literature. Add scissors, paper bags, paste, buttons, and scraps of fabrics, and you're all ready for rollicking evenings of fun. And the hours invested pay off rich dividends in future fun every time the puppets are used. A puppet performance may be staged by one child, changing puppets as the story progresses, or children may be assigned to one puppet each. The story may be narrated by a reader or each puppeteer may speak his own lines.

A simple puppet theater can be created by hanging a sheet or a piece of cardboard across a doorway extending a couple of inches above the performer's heads. Or a table on its side makes a good shield for performers holding their puppets aloft.

Let's start with "Goldilocks and the Three Bears." Paper bags size eight are just right for Mama Bear and Papa Bear, size six for Goldilocks, and size four for Baby Bear. As indicated in the illustrations, the folded bottom of the bag becomes the head, with the mouth at the edge of the fold. This permits the appearance of a mouth which opens and closes to indicate talking when the puppet is manipulated by a hand inside the sack. Note that the major part of the tongue is under the fold so that it shows best when the puppet "speaks." (The hand opens inside the sack.)

Faces, hands, and feet of the bears are made of imitation fur fabric, pasted to the bag. Buttons are used for eyes and nose, and the tongues are red felt. Shirts for Papa and Baby Bear are solid color fabrics, with overalls of bright plaid. Mama Bear's dress is gingham print with a plain color organdy apron added.

The high points are reached in the puppet performance of this great favorite when each of the bears in turn reaches the "my" in lines such as "Someone's been sitting in *my* chair."

The face and legs of Goldilocks are of flesh-colored paper. Her hair consists of several strands of iridescent crinkled gift ribbon. These and other puppets in this section are adapted with permission from designs by Rissa Clarke.

Puppets for the Story of the "Little Red Hen"

This favorite children's "Do it myself" story becomes a lively action play with the addition of colorful sack puppets. If you need help in remembering the story, encourage your children to look up the story in a reference book in your home or at the local library. A lovely interpretation for child action, including pictures, rhymes and songs is contained in Ginn and Company's publication *The Kindergarten Book* by Pitts, Glenn, and Walters.

The puppets shown here are made of colored construction paper mounted on tagboard or cardboard from a manila file folder, pasted on a size eight paper bag to fit the hand and produce mouth action.

Red hen:
　　Body—red.
　　Apron and sash—white with blue dots.
　　Feet, beak, eyes and comb—yellow.
　　Mouth interior (under sack flap)—red,
　　　with yellow lower beak.

Cat:
　　Body and head—black.
　　Eyes—green.
　　Nose, mouth, and tongue—pink.

Pig:
Body—white or cream, with black spots.
Nose—pink.
(Using other colors, the same design
may be utilized for making puppets
for the "Three Little Pigs" story.)

Frog:
Body—light green.
Legs and head—olive or dark green.
Inside mouth—pink.
Eyes—white with black pupils.

Puppets for "The Gingerbread Man"

This much-loved story comes to life with the use of sack puppets, pasted on size eight paper bags. Tagboard is again used to back up the colored construction paper. Real fabrics can be pasted on as clothing for the little old lady and the little old man.

Gingerbread man:
    Face, hands, trousers and shoes—tan.
    Shirt—brown.
    Hair, collar, cuffs, buttons—pink.
    Lips and tongue—red.

Little old lady:
    Hair and face—tagboard, colored with
        water colors or crayons.
    Dress—light blue or light green with
        pink flowers.
    Apron—yellow.

Little old man:
    Hair and face—tagboard, colored with
        watercolors or crayons.
    Shirt—red.
    Overalls—blue.

Rabbit:
Gray—Furry fabric can be pasted on.
Nose and inside ears—pink.
Tongue—red.

Fox:
Head and body—brown.
Mouth, tongue, and nose—red.
Eyes—green, with black pupils.
Eyelashes—yellow.

Cow:
Head and body—tan with brown spots.
Mouth, nostrils, and inside ears—pink.
Daisy—yellow or cream with brown center.

The fox can do double duty as the wolf in the story of the "Three Little Pigs." The fox puppet and the hen puppet can also be used in telling the story of the hen who took scissors from her apron pocket and cut the bag into which the fox had placed her. She substituted a stone in the bag, and when the fox poured the bag's contents into a pot of boiling water, the stone splashed scalding water on the fox and he never bothered the hen again.

Peter Rabbit Stories:

The rabbit puppet from the cast of "The Gingerbread Man" can be used to dramatize the many enthralling Peter Rabbit stories. For Peter's relatives, use the same pattern in other colors and sizes. The "little old man" makes a good Farmer McGregor. Other sack puppet characters from this section can be used: cat, girl, boy, fox.

"Ask Mr. Bear" story *

This delightful story by Marjorie Flack is excellent for dramatization by young puppeteers. Danny, searching for a birthday present for his mother, consults his animal friends and is offered things which his mother already has. The Hen offers an egg; the Goose could give feathers for a pillow. Cheese is offered by the Goat, and then the Sheep expresses willingness to give some wool for a blanket. The Cow proffers milk and cream, then suggests that Danny ask Mr. Bear.

Mr. Bear whispers a suggestion in Danny's ear which sends him running eagerly home to have his mother guess. She tries to guess all the possibilities mentioned by the animals and finally gets her present—a Big Birthday Bear Hug.

The sack puppets are of tagboard or manila folders, made lively with construction paper or fabric.

Danny:
Face, neck, and arms—pink.
Shirt—yellow.
Trousers—blue.

* The Macmillan Co. Reprinted in *Time For Fairy Tales*, Scott, Foresman, and Co.

Sheep:
 Wool—white.
 Cheeks and inside ears—pink.
 Tongue—red.

Goat:
 Head and body—white with black spots.
 Eyes—gray.
 Tongue and inside ears—pink.

Bear:
 Body and head—brown.
 Tie—yellow.
 Nose and inside ears—dark brown.
 Eyes—brown with light brown outline.

Mother:
 Use "Little Old Lady" from "Gingerbread Man."

Hen:
 Use "Little Red Hen" puppet.

Goose:
 Use duck from "Little White Duck."

Cow:
 Use cow from "Little Red Hen."

Angus and the Ducks *

Here is another popular story by Marjorie Flack which lends itself well to dramatization with sack puppets as visual aids.

Angus:
 Head and body—tan.
 Tongue—red.

Ducks:
 Use several like the one described in "Little White Duck."

Little White Duck Sitting on the Water

This lilting children's song becomes a lively action song with the use of sack puppets.

There's a little white duck,
 sitting on the water.
A little white duck,
 doing what he oughter.
A little white duck, sitting on the water,
Quack! Quack! Quack!
 Duck:
 Head and body—white.
 Feet and bill—orange.
 Eyes—yellow.

* Doubleday and Co., Inc., Reprinted in *Time for True Tales*, Scott, Foresman, and Co.

There's a little green snake,
  swimming in the water,
etc. etc.
Hiss, hiss, hiss.

Snake:
  Head and body—green.
  Tongue—red.
  Eyes—yellow.

There's a little red bug,
  floating on the water.
etc. etc.
Buzz, buzz, buzz.

Bug:
  Body and head—black.
  Face—yellow.
  Lips and tongue—red.
  Wings—orange with black dots and yellow edge.
  Eyes—green.

The Little Engine That Could

The sack puppet illustrated here can be used in many stories involving trains along with others of the sack puppets illustrated above and below.

Train:
  Body and face—black.
  Cowcatcher and smoke—gray.
  Face outline—yellow.
  Tongue—red.

Clown:
> Body, feet, arms, and hat—purple.
> Ruffles, buttons, nose, and hatbrim—
> pink.
> Face, teeth and collar—white.
> Mustache, eyes, and eyebrows—black.

Rooster:
> Body and head—cream.
> Feet and beak—orange.
> Comb, wattles, and outer eye circles—
> red.
> Tail, inner feathers—cream;
> intermediate feathers—brown;
> outside feathers—orange.

Dog:
> Use "Angus" puppet.

Christopher Robin and Winnie-the-Pooh

Using the sack puppets previously illustrated, a group of children may improvise numbers of characters from the Pooh stories:

> Christopher Robin: Boy puppet, page 74.
> Piglet: Pig Puppet, page 71
> Pooh: Bear puppet, page 75.
> Rabbit: Peter Rabbit puppet, page 73.

Eeyore:
   Head and body gray.
   Mane and tail—black.
   Inside ears—pink.
   Tongue—red.
   Eyes—yellow.
Owl:
   Head and body—tan.
   Feet and beak—yellow.
   Eyes—green.
   Tongue—red.

For more creative experience and realistic production, the children can paint backdrops and make movable scenery props for the stories.

Bibliography: The following A. A. Milne books, illustrated by E. H. Shepard, are published by E. P. Dutton and Co., Inc., 286 Fourth Ave., New York 10. *When We Were Very Young. Winnie-the-Pooh. The House at Poor Corner. Now We Are Six.*

"The World of Pooh Lives On" is a six-page section in *Life* magazine for February 27, 1956, included to commemorate the death of A. A. Milne.

Records: "Winnie-the-Pooh Songs" by A. A. Milne and H. Fraser-Simson, vocal-orchestra (Decca Record 78 rpm CU-109; 45 rpm 1-148).

"Winnie-the-Pooh and Eeyore," narrated by Jimmy Stewart, music by Norman Leyden; opposite side—"Kanga and Baby Roo" (Victor Record No. 47-0288).

"Winnie the Pooh and Tigger" and "Winnie the Pooh and the Heffalump," narrated by Jimmy Stewart, with a picture-story book; price $3.57 (order from Children's Music Center, 2858 W. Pico Boulevard, Los Angeles 6, California).

Improvising Sack Puppets for Other Stories

With the puppets illustrated here, children can dramatize many of the stories in their own books, sometimes using the puppets as they are, or perhaps modifying a puppet with a change of costume. With this start in making stories come to life for viewing and hearing, the children may enjoy creating sack puppets to portray other favorite storybook characters.

The following books from the library or bookstore will help children and parents who are interested in expanding their puppet knowledge and skills:

Let's Make A Puppet, Helen Farnune and Blanche Wheeler
A Handbook of First Puppets, Bessie A. Ficklen
The Extra Curricular Library: Puppet Plays, Collins and Charlton
Marionettes—A Hobby for Everyone, Mabel and Les Beaton
Childcraft has a good section on puppets, Volume 8

Paper Bag Masks

Paper bags also make wonderful masks for Halloween, a circus, plays, or for just plain creative fun. First place the sack over the head and crumple the paper where eyes, nose, and mouth should be cut to fit properly. Then cut the openings and draw the designs desired.

Noses should be slightly larger than the opening cut in the paper to facilitate good gluing. Add life with colored paper features.

11.

Curtain Time!

DRAMA AND ITS RELATED ARTS CAN OPEN UP A WHOLE NEW world to a family interested in broadening its horizons. Of course, there is no substitute for the legitimate theater, and families should take advantage of every opportunity to see a stage play. If your community doesn't have a theater which sponsors professional productions, there may be amateur groups—either at the high school or college level—who produce good plays. Or perhaps a little theater group sponsored by a church or civic organization can provide the opportunity for viewing a play.

There is something magical about the curtain going up, the colorful settings, and the stage design, the responsive audience, the action of the players, and the interpretation of the actor's role that is impossible to capture any other way.

However, if it isn't possible to see good play productions in your community, this doesn't mean your family can't have many exciting hours listening to good drama. You will find it a most pleasant evening if you get a copy of a good play and assign members of the family to read specific parts with as much feeling and interpretation as possible.

One of the advantages of play reading at home is that you can concentrate on the play and forget the complication of getting tickets in advance, rushing to get to the theater on time, parking cars, and hiring baby sitters. When you enjoy drama at home, the play is ready when you are.

When you read plays, one of the rewards is that you can concentrate more fully on the dramatist and his ideas. Reading the words will often stimulate a good discussion among the readers. Another advantage of reading drama is that you can repeat passages that are difficult or full of meaning. Of course, reading a play doesn't take precedence over seeing a first-rate production, but listening to a great play can be more rewarding than seeing a mediocre one. You may enjoy inviting other families of friends to join with you for an evening of drama.

Drama on Records

For those families who thoroughly enjoy good drama at home, and who would like to increase their understanding and knowledge of drama, records of great plays featuring the world's best actors are now available. These cover the entire panorama of drama from Euripides to the present day.

Judith Anderson's recording of Euripides' *Medea* (Decca 9000) is electrifying. Sophocles' *Antigone* (Folkway 9861) and *Oedipus Rex* (Caedmon 2012) are stunningly contemporary in their insight and both worthy of your attention, especially if you haven't seen or heard these before. The record companies skip from the Greeks to the Elizabethan period with Christopher Marlowe's play *Doctor Faustus* (Caedmon 1033).

Shakespeare, of course, has attracted the widest audiences and you'll be thrilled with the magnificent Shakespearean records. Thirty of these records are available, among the best of which are *The Merchant of Venice* with Michael Redgrave (Caedmon TC-2013), *Hamlet* with John Gielgud (Victor LM6404), *Othello* with Paul Robeson and Jose Ferrer (Columbia SL153), and *Macbeth* with Alec Guinness (Victor LM6010).

The Irish playwrights are represented by John Millington Synge's *The Playboy of the Western World* (Angel 3547B) and Sean O'Casey's *Juno and the Paycock* (Angel 3540). Oscar Wilde's *The Importance of Being Earnest* (Angel 3540B) has probably the most scintillating cast on records, starring John Gielgud, Edith Evans, and

Pamela Brown. George Bernard Shaw is represented on records by *Don Juan in Hell* (Columbia USL166) played by Charles Boyer, Charles Laughton, Agnes Moorehead, and Sir Cedric Hardwicke. Christopher Fry's *The Lady's Not for Burning* (Decca DX110) is a philosophical romp featuring John Gielgud and Pamela Brown. Arthur Miller's *Death of a Salesman* (Decca DXA102) stars Thomas Mitchell as the tragic Willy Lohman. T. S. Eliot's *Murder in the Cathedral* (Angel 3505B) was never written as a conventional play but is a forceful drama with Robert Donat and the other players from the Old Vic portraying the political murder of Archbishop Thomas á Beckett.

Home Grown Drama

One of the finest of all spontaneous family night activities is a home-grown, home-produced evening of drama. Acting out plays, stories and nursery rhymes gives children and adults an opportunity to express themselves in many ways. If the children are young, they can begin by acting out simple nursery rhyme characters such as Jack and Jill, Little Bo-Peep, Humpty-Dumpty, and so on. The nursery stories about the "Three Little Pigs," "The Three Bears," and "The Three Billie Goats Gruff" are delightfully easy to act out since they are well known and only require four characters for the cast. Simple props and costumes can be devised by the children and will add to the fun. Goldilocks just needs long golden hair made from yellow crêpe paper or yarn. The three goats can sport cotton tufts of beards, while the troll wears a grotesque paper-sack mask. Cone-shaped paper cups tied to the head make wonderful ears or horns. You will be surprised at how original and creative children can be with a little encouragement. The entire family can have fun dramatizing stories using the simple paper-sack puppets illustrated on the previous pages.

There are many one-act plays that can be presented in a family theater. Older children will enjoy producing them. Many of these plays are written for small casts such as an average family might provide.

Your family will gain much pleasure if you read aloud on a February night Maxwell Anderson's stirring play *Valley Forge* published by Samuel French, 25 West 45th St., New York City. The Samuel B.

French Co. and the Hansen Novelty Co. both publish catalogues of plays that will be helpful if you are looking for material. *The Christmas Book* (National Recreation Association, 315 Fourth Ave., New York City) will also provide seasonal dramas.

Other books that will be worthwhile to the family interested in drama are *Dramatization of Bible Stories* by Elizabeth Miller (Chicago University Press) and *Off-Stage* a book on how to make plays from books you read, written by Marguerite Fellows Malcher and published by Knopf.

If your family has a flair for the dramatic, try writing down some of your family experiences, especially the humorous ones. Then re-enact them for the family theater. Almost any incident in story or song can make a scene for the theater.

Choral reading is coming back to popularity and your next family hour might well feature a dramatic reading of passages from *John Brown's Body* by Stephen Vincent Benet or G. B. Shaw's *Man and Superman*. Selections of poetry, great prose passages from classic writings, selections from the Bible or from famous plays also make good choral reading. You will want to preview the selection you choose and note passages to be solo parts, duets, or ensemble readings. This activity is challenging and stimulating to the family who enjoys the dramatic arts and can be rewarding to the family who hasn't heretofore tried this field for talent.

12.

Sharing the Pleasures of Music

At a very early age children begin to enjoy the sounds and rhythms of music and it is a wise parent who encourages and develops this interest. Very young children are sensitive to the charms of songs, including lullabys and nonsense songs familiar to most parents.

Noises and children seem to go together, and very young children will enjoy beating out rhythms with a drum or baton to the accompaniment of music. Control can be taught by teaching children to beat fast or slow, loud or soft, smooth or jumpy.

One of the joys of music is in helping children and adults explain their feelings. Music can help get rid of bottled-up feelings. It can make one feel sad, happy, frightened, angry, gay, or solemn. A music program in the home can be ever changing and of infinite variety. Songs, because they are absorbed without effort, also help increase children's vocabularies and information. Music in the background can help set a mood and add interest to a dramatization. For example, if you are portraying the Three Bears walking through the woods, use a smooth rhythm. But as Goldilocks comes skipping along, change to a light, lively tune.

The Children Sing

If you wish to bring out the best in a child, get him to sing. Singing in the home is fostered through singing familiar songs with children. Encourage your children to sing with you, and for you, especially songs they have learned in school, church, or elsewhere. If the stage is set properly for a family hour of song, children will become increasingly interested in singing for one another and they may develop into an excellent ensemble.

Folk music is one kind of music that families can enjoy together. Children will enjoy the pattern of such light operatic works as Gilbert and Sullivan's, and folk songs of all kinds. No child is too young or too old to enjoy the rollicking nonsense of "Nick Nack Paddy Whack," "Polly Wolly Doodle," or "A Frog He Would a-Wooing Go." These songs are easy to learn and hard to forget. Everyone can be an arranger or interpreter of folk songs, for there is no "right" way to sing them. The variations possible are part of the charm of folk music. You can add new words and new sounds to suit your mood and talents. Background sounds are lots of fun and add music interest. For example, when singing "I've Been Working on the Railroad," have part of the children chant the train sounds, such as chug-chug-chug, in the background while others sing the words and melody. "In a Clock Shop" and "Grandfather's Clock" are interesting music story records that can also use background sounds or choruses.

Folk songs are fun to sing when traveling or when going on walks. "I Am a Happy Wanderer," "I've Got Sixpence," and the Scout "Hiking Song" are wonderful cadence songs that lift the spirits as you stride along.

Many excellent sources are available with songs for children. *American Folk Songs For Children* by Ruth Crawford Seegar (Doubleday) and *Songs to Grow On* and *More Songs to Grow On* by Beatrice Landeck (Marks-Sloane) are outstanding songbooks for children with good Christmas carol collections. The *Fireside Book of Folk Songs* edited by Margaret Boni (Simon and Schuster) is an excellent family collection of songs containing ballads, hymns and spirituals, cowboy songs, folk songs, and Christmas carols. If you would like to start a collection of good folk songs, here is a list of several inexpensive song books:

Burl Ives Song Book—Ballantine Books—50¢

Girl Scout Song Book—Girl Scouts, Inc., 14 W. 49th St., New York.

Animal Folk Songs for Children, Ruth Crawford Seegar—Doubleday Co., Inc., Garden City, New York.

God's Wonderful World, Mason and Chanian—Signet Key Books —50¢

Treasury of Folk Songs, edited by Koeh—Bantum Books (#A1227) —35¢

Your family will have a great time learning these novel songs. Some of them have delightful actions to accompany them.

ORCHESTRA ACTION SONG

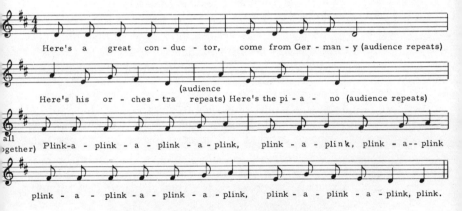

ORCHESTRA ACTION SONG

I. Here's a great conductor, come from Germany (audience repeats)
Here's his orchestra (audience repeats)

Here's the piano (audience repeats)
(All together, making piano action with hands)

(A) Plink-a-plink-a-plink-a-plink
Plink-a-plink, plink-a-plink,
Plink-a-plink-a-plink-a-plink
Plink-a-plink-a-plink, plink.

Repeat I

Here's the viola (audience repeats)

(All together making actions of viola with arms)

(B) Vee-o-vee-o-vee-o-la
Vee-o-la, vee-o-la,
Vee-o-vee-o-vee-o-la
Vee-o-vee-o-la, la.   (Then all repeat A)

Repeat I

Here is the snare drum (audience repeats)

(All together, making drum action with arms)

(C) Ra-ta-ta-ta-ta-ta-ta,
etc.   (Then all repeat B and A)

Repeat I

Here is the bagpipe (audience repeats)

(All together, holding nose with left hand and gently tapping above Adam's apple with right hand, in rhythm to music)

(D) Aa-aa-aa-aa-aa-aa-aa (nasal sound)
etc.   (Then all repeat C, B and A)

Repeat I

Here is the tuba (audience repeats)

(All together, placing thumbs under armpits and moving elbows outward and upward in rhythm—up for "oom," down for "pah")

(E) Oompah-oompah-oompah-pah,
Oompah-pah, etc.   (Then all repeat D, C, B and A)

Other instruments may be improvised, such as:
French Horn: Toodle-oodle-oodle-oo
Flute: Tweedle-eedle-eedle-ee
Trombone: Tromble-omble-omble-om
Timpani: Pompom-pompom-pompom-pom

Repeat I

Here's the conductor (audience repeats)

(F) (All together, make motions of conducting while silently running the tune through the mind.)
(Then all repeat E, D, C, B and A)

Repeat I
> Here is the audience (audience repeats)
> (All together, clap to rhythm of music)
> (G) Clap-clap, clap-clap, clap-clap, clap, etc.
>> (Then all repeat F, E, D, C, B and A)

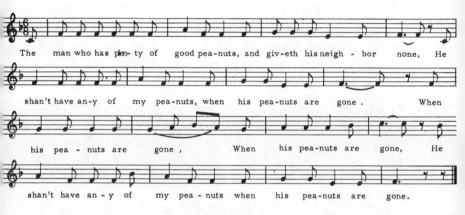

"PEANUTS"   TONGUE - TWISTER SONG

The man who has plen-ty of good pea-nuts, and giv-eth his neigh-bor none, He shan't have an-y of my pea-nuts, when his pea-nuts are gone. When his pea-nuts are gone, When his pea-nuts are gone, He shan't have an-y of my pea-nuts when his pea-nuts are gone.

"PEANUTS"

Tongue-Twister Song

1. The man who has plenty of *good peanuts*,
   And giveth his neighbor none,
   He shan't have any of my *peanuts*
   When his *peanuts* are gone.

   When his *peanuts* are gah-ah-ah-ahn,
   When his *peanuts* are gone,
   He shan't have any of my *peanuts*
   When his *peanuts* are gone.

(In other verses, substitute the following phrases in place of italicized phrases above:)

2. Soft sweet soda crackers.
3. Nice rich red ripe strawberry shortcake.

4. Saint Jacob's oil for rheumatism, corns, cramps, chaps, chatters, and chilblains.
5. Demonitized demoralized degenerate unconstitutional sappinacious silver money.
6. John Wanamaker's reversible revisible double-them-up-and-sit-on-them operatic plug hats. (Then sing the song through, using "good peanuts" in the first line, "soft sweet soda crackers" in second line, etc., and "peanuts" in last line.)

Opera

Your family will have a good time trying its hand—or voice—at opera. Not grand, of course, but still it's opera. Take any familiar story and set it to your own music. For example, "The Vermilion Riding Cloak" commonly known as "Little Red Riding Hood" is a good one to try. Cast the parts and have a very brief rehearsal. Simple masks and costumes will add to the fun! Little Red Riding Hood wears a hood of red, Grandma wears a flannel night gown and cap, the wolf wears a mask left over from Halloween, and the woodsman carries an ax. You might want to have someone be the narrator and read the lines between "arias."

Act I

Mother is waving goodbye to her little darling Red Riding Hood who is going to visit her grandma who lives in the woods. With deep emotion you hear her farewell aria as she sings:
"Goodnight, Sweetheart"

Act II

Deep in the forest we find Little Red Riding Hood as she happily goes her way singing:
"I'm off to see my grandma, my grandma"
She is overtaken by the mean, old wolf who entices her by singing:
"Come to my *adobe hacienda*"
She looks at him in horror as she answers:
"No, no a thousand times no"
The wolf is very insulted and so he proudly walks off singing:
"I know that someday you'll want me to want you"

And Red Riding Hood goes her merry way, picking the flowers
along the path.

Act III

The wolf has arrived at grandma's house in the middle of the
forest and is knocking at the door. Grandma is heard singing:
"Who's that knocking at my door?"
The wolf throws open the door and sings:
"I want what I want when I want it"
He bounds over to the bed, gobbles up Grandma, and sings:
"Good, good, good, that's you, that's you"
The wolf puts on Grandma's hat and gets into bed to wait for
Little Red. She arrives singing:
"Open the door, Granny"
She comes in and goes over to the wolf. As she sees him she sings:
"Jeepers Creepers, where'd you get those peepers?"
The wolf jumps up and Red Riding Hood is frantic. She sings
out:
"Give me a man who's a stout-hearted man—*any man*"
The handsome woodsman comes and kills the wolf, and he and
Red Riding Hood sing:
"Come, come, I love you only."

A Family Orchestra

To enrich your family's appreciation and understanding of music,
use every opportunity to let the family, especially the children, see,
hear, touch, feel, and blow any instrument you can find. And by all
means, encourage the children to play an instrument as soon as possible if they show the slightest inclination or talent. For even though
the child may never be a virtuoso, familiarity with an instrument
will increase interest in music and provide an opportunity for that
child to contribute something to the family's musical talent. Nothing
can bring about a finer feeling for beauty and harmony in the home
than a choice instrumental solo or ensemble played by members of
the family. Encourage the musical talent in your family with every
resource available to help the child gain the technique necessary to
achieve proficiency on an instrument. Encourage the children to join
the school band as early as possible. This association with other

musicians will give valuable experience and confidence. Many schools have musical instruments they loan or rent to beginning students.

Milton Cross has produced a series of records called "Learn for Pleasure" in which the instruments of the orchestra are explained. He has also produced the "Magic of Music" series which is fun and instructive. Your family, especially the children, will enjoy these records very much, and they will help you in your quest for better music awareness.

Playing a simple musical instrument such as a recorder, guitar, ukulele, or auto harp will encourage and improve the musical talent within the family. These instruments are fairly simple to play and can be mastered without too much talent or effort. An auto harp, popular with folk-singers, is not an expensive instrument and makes a perfect background accompaniment for family singing. It is fairly easy to play and has a lovely tone.

One family we know has had a marvelous time since they started playing the recorder as a family project. They spend many hours together practicing and improvising musical numbers for their own pleasure as well as for others. All of them, even the younger children, have become quite proficient.

The recorder is an ideal family instrument because it is fairly inexpensive. It requires almost no musical background to learn to play, and yet it offers enough range and possibilities to tempt even the most professional musician.

Beginning with the highest pitched instrument and smallest in size and going on down to the lowest pitched and largest in size, they are the sopranino, soprano, alto, tenor, and bass. The soprano is probably played by the most people with the alto second. A soprano ranges in price from about $10 to $26. A sopranino is a little less. The others are gradually higher priced according to size.

A good beginning instruction book is *Enjoy Your Recorder* by the Trapp Family Singers, Magnamusic Distributors Inc., Sharon, Connecticut ($1.50).

Nothing can take the place of a real live concert or performance if you want to enlarge your family's musical experience. So as often as the budget will allow, take the family to whatever musical events are available in your area. Attend the symphony or a chamber music recital. In a live performance the personalities of the musicians and the program content provide stimulation and appreciation of the music.

Not everyone responds to music in the same way. It may be that your family will enjoy a ballet or an opera better than a symphony. Sometimes a ballet or an opera performance with dancing and drama will make a familiar musical score more vivid.

An excellent book that is related closely to musicology is A *Dictionary of Ballet* by G. B. L. Wilson (Penguin), 95¢. This book contains a thorough lexicography of ballet including important people, places, and events. It includes technical terms and phrases, sketches of ballet positions and forms, a brief history of the great ballet companies, and outlines of many ballets included in the most popular repertoires.

The summer season is a wonderful time to increase children's participation in a cultural life. Many of the best musical offerings of the year are sponsored during the summer months. Summer opera, summer theater groups, summer stock, concerts, and shows are presented in areas all over the country and frequently these productions are held in cool, quiet, refreshing places where it is a real joy to spend a summer afternoon or evening with your family. Plan to include these programs in your summer schedule and you'll be delighted at how much children will enjoy the events, especially if they have had a little beforehand preparation. If you can, listen to recordings of the music to be played before you attend the concert.

The record industry has opened up the whole world of music to the listener who enjoys good music of every kind. It may not always be possible to take the family to a live performance of music by a great artist or group of artists, but you can bring the world's greatest musicians into your home via the recording arts.

In addition to playing the recordings and becoming familiar with the music itself, a short biography of the composers' lives will often appeal to children. If your own background doesn't include familiarity with music and musicians, you may find a few source books helpful. Howard Taubman's *How to Bring Up Your Child to Enjoy Music* is highly recommended, as are Leonard Bernstein's TV programs. Several paperback books are available which can be used for references, including books by Aaron Copland, Carter Harmon and Oscar Thompson.

A very inexpensive music library for your home can be found among the paperback editions of music reference books. For a very nominal fee, under $15.00, you can have a basic reference library with a wide range of interests. These books will answer nearly any question you have about music and if you read them, you will learn a great deal about this fascinating art and its creators. Music critics recommend *A Popular History of Music* by Carter Harmon, published by Dell (50¢). This is an engrossing volume that covers an amazingly wide range of interest and includes diagrams such as what the instruments of an orchestra look like and the construction of an organ. *Men of Music* by Brockway & Weinstock (Simon & Schuster, $1.95) is another fine book containing biographies of the significant composers in the history of music. They are portrayed as human beings as well as musical geniuses, men without whom there would be no music as we know it today.

Penguin Books have a series of several volumes pertaining to music. *The Music Masters* comprise four volumes. These histories, biographies, and essays cover the entire range of music from the 16th century to the 20th century. Three additional Penguin volumes related to the symphony, the concerto, and chamber music are also available for 85¢ to 95¢ each.

The Book of Jazz by Leonard Feather (Meridian, $1.35) puts the emphasis on the instruments, the men who play them, and the structure of the music. A section on improvisation gives an explanation of the essence of jazz music and what makes it sound the way it does. Another section includes the part each instrument has played in the development of jazz music and an exposition of the most famous performers on each instrument from the beginning of jazz to the present.

13.

Living Room Journeys

It is fun for the family to take an imaginary trip to Mexico, Hawaii, Norway, or Spain, so why not plan a series of family night programs around various countries you'd like to know more about? Give the program a real flourish by having an appropriate menu from the country to be visited that particular month. Many recipes for foreign foods can be found in magazines. We have found *Sunset* magazine's "Cooking With a Foreign Accent" indispensible.

After dinner you can consult a map or a globe and trace the journey you will take to get to your chosen country. On a subsequent family night you can profitably spend the time discussing manners and customs of the country, music and composers, folk songs and dances, and games that are favorites of that particular country. Reference books or the library will provide much of this material.

A good program to follow is to choose one country to study each month. Then once a week, on your family evening program, devote the time to learning about the country you have chosen. For example, on the first week you might begin by serving appropriate food at the dinner hour. Then study the map of the country to become acquainted with its location and geographical features. On the map, trace a possible journey from your home to the new country and learn interesting information concerning historical sights and other attractive features you would like to know about.

On the second week be prepared to discuss interesting costumes, manners, and customs. Read something about the country's history and famous people, either real or fictitious.

On the third week you can play or sing music of the chosen country, paying extra attention to the lives of famous composers and musicians. Play their compositions. Learn a few of the native folksongs and sing them, or learn a simple native folk dance. The "World of Fun" records are a good investment for a family who would like to learn native folk dances.

On the fourth and last week read from the literature of the country, or discuss famous books which have that country for their locale.

Here are the ways in which five far lands were visited, in a manner of speaking, by families we know.

The Family Takes a Trip to Turkey *

Turkey is a fascinating country where old and new, living side by side, do not understand each other.

The present country of Turkey was formerly known as the Ottoman Empire and has been for centuries the crossroad of the eastern and western worlds. Its former capital, Istanbul (which used to be called Constantinople and long before that Byzantium), is the only capital in the world that spanned two continents and the only place in the world where one can go by boat from one continent to another for 5¢. The present capital is Ankara. Find Turkey on a map and study it.

In Istanbul there are 500 mosques, 25 of these are very big ones. Here the people go to pray. At the entrance they must wash their hands, face and feet, and then they enter the mosque without shoes. There are no chairs or benches. The people kneel on the floor. Look up more about the Islam religion and its founder, Mohammed.

There are modern schools in the cities. However, 80% of the people live in very small isolated villages as they did hundreds of years ago. About 40% of the villages have no schools. In the cities many women dress as we do in America, but face veils are still worn by women in the villages.

To the poor villager the little donkey is his most valuable possession. It carries his burdens and is his only means of transportation over the dusty and muddy roads. At an early age the little girls learn embroidery. The boys take the little flocks of sheep and goats out

* Written by MRS. MARK K. ALLEN

in the hills and herd them all day. For lunch they have a loaf of heavy brownish bread and perhaps some onions.

Did you know:

1. That King Midas of the Golden Touch was a real king of Phrygia and lived on the Citadel in what is now Ankara. Tell the story of King Midas.

2. That the original Santa Claus was born in Myra in Southern Turkey. His bones are in a case in a museum in Antalya. Look up the story about him.

3. That over 50 places mentioned in the Bible are in Turkey.

   a. Mt. Ararat where Noah's Ark came to rest is in Eastern Turkey.

   b. Tarsus where St. Paul was born is in Turkey.

   c. Ephesus where St. John and St. Luke were buried is in Turkey.

   Perhaps you can find some of the other places in Turkey that are mentioned in the Bible.

4. That the children of Turkey do not have toys as children have in America. One thing they like to do is to make figures out of paper and have a "shadow play" by holding these figures between a light and a sheet of white paper. Try this on your family night.

5. That the Turkish people would never think of having a baby sitter come in. They wouldn't trust a stranger to stay with their children.

6. That the Turkish people love their flag and display it every weekend on all government buildings. These flags are huge and cover the entire side of a building. The field is colored red, and the crescent and star are yellow.

7. That the ancient city of Troy was in Turkey. Read the story of Helen of Troy.

Today there are many Americans in Turkey because that government has asked for our help in agriculture, engineering, education, and in many other fields.

A Family Night Visit to Friends in Mexico *

This week, for our family night fun, how about visiting "South of the Border, Down Mexico Way."

* Written by MRS. CREED BRIMHALL

The Mexican people are a very interesting people. Most of them live very simple lives. They do not have many things to make life easy as we do. Many of them live in small adobe homes they have built themselves. Many are farmers with very small farms. No matter how rich or poor the people are, they all love very bright colors. This is reflected in their clothes. Reds and blues seem to be the favorite. Most people in Mexico have a siesta, which is a long rest period at mid-day. The businesses and stores close up and the farmers stop working for about two hours each day right after lunch.

The Mexicans love for bright colors is shown in their table settings. They use very bright cloths and colorful pottery. Your children could make some bright table mats out of construction paper. Use these while serving a Mexican dinner. You could have tacos, tamales, enchiladas, or chili con carne. Serve with a green salad and fresh fruit for dessert.

It would also be fun to make a piñata. These are clay pots filled with goodies. The people use these for all kinds of celebrations. You can make yours out of a large paper sack. Fill the sack with scraps of paper until it holds a shape. Twist the top a number of times making it look like a long neck. Wrap the bag with strips of white, fringed crêpe paper. Add a few extra ruffles for a tail, use pipe cleaners for feet, yellow paper for a bill, and you have a duck. Many other animals can be made by using the large sack as a base. You may want to put candy or nuts into the piñata so when you break it the children scramble to get them.

Let's include singing a Mexican song. Here are a few: "El Rancho Grande," "La Cucaracha," and "South of the Border."

Here are a few Spanish words that would be fun to know and use:

peso—dollar	hoy—today
adios—goodbye	rio—river
casa—house	dos—two
tres—three	cinco—five
mañana—tomorrow	uno—one
hola—hello	cuatro—four

muchas gracias—many thanks

The Family Visits Friends in France

Here you are all dressed up in a new beret bought from an artist in France. Why don't you get your palette and color the French Flag which is known as the Tri-color. The colors are written in French. Can you figure them out? Bleu, Blanc, Rouge.

Paris is the capital of France. It is one of the most beautiful cities in the world. It is located on the Seine River. A favorite landmark in Paris is the Eiffel Tower; built in 1899 for the World's Fair, it was at that time the tallest building in the world.

France is famous as an art center, and no one should go to Paris without a visit to the Louvre Museum, which holds many of the world's priceless art treasures. Try to find a copy of da Vinci's "Mona Lisa," and study it. It is perhaps the most famous of all paintings, and the original is in the Louvre.

Besides art, Paris is famous as the fashion center of the world. Ask mother if she would like to have a special gown made especially for her by a French designer.

If you visit in the summer, you could go with friends to the French Riviera. It is located on the coast of the Mediterranean Sea, and is one of the world's most beautiful beaches.

In winter you would enjoy skiing on the slopes of Mont Blanc, the highest mountain in the Alps, stretching up some 15,781 feet.

Perhaps the most popular sport in France is cycling. The annual bicycle race through France has as many enthusiastic fans as we have in the United States for the World Series.

Another thing the French people are noted for is their cooking. Many of our words used often in regard to food come from the French language. *Restaurant* is a French word, and when you go there you might see a *chef* in a tall hat fixing a *casserole*, or preparing potatoes *au gratin*, or serving you some pie *à la mode*. Just for fun for family night, serve some *Crêpe Suzettes*. Have mother stir some pancake mix with two eggs and enough milk to have the batter very thin. Pour about one-half cup on a griddle. Turn carefully and when done, put on a dinner plate and sprinkle with sifted powdered sugar, spread with jelly, then roll up. Add a little more sugar on top and you are eating a real French pancake.

Here are a few famous French names. See if you can identify them; if not, look them up: LaFayette, Napoleon, Jeanne d'Arc, DeGaulle.

Ask Dad to tell you about the Palace of Versailles and why it is important in our own history. Maybe Mother can tell you about the Statue of Liberty. Sing a little song in French about Brother John, *Frère Jacques*.

A few French words you can easily learn are:

bon jour—good day   merci beaucoup—thank you very much
au revoir—goodbye   mes amis—my friends

Foreign Languages

While you are studying foreign countries at home on your family evening programs, you will enjoy learning a few of the words used in France, Spain, or Germany. One painless and delightful way, as well as scientifically sound, to learn a foreign language is listening to language teaching records. Studies show a new language should be introduced by first hearing it and then by speaking it. The records have the advantage of giving you a perfect accent to imitate and you can play them over and over until they are mastered.

You can play the records at mealtime, as a background while you are all doing family chores such as dishwashing or ironing, or while bathing. Children are especially adept at picking up words and phrases and will soon imitate the words they hear.

A fifteen minute period set aside each day for studying a new language will reap rewards later on and can be the beginning of a fascinating program that will carry over during the years to come. There are many song books and records available to assist you in your study and at the same time nurture the children's interest in other people. "Songs in French for Children" (Columbia), "Folk Songs for Children of all Ages in Spanish" (Cantenos), "Songs Children Sing in Italy" (Judson), and "Israel Folk Songs" (Folkways), are all lively changes from the songs you usually hear and will aid in developing a child's sense of melody and the sound of a language.

As your family's vocabulary increases, you will enjoy reading foreign language books, newspapers and magazines. These are available in all stages of language abilities from *Peter Rabbit* to *Doctor Zhivago*. *The Big Golden Book Dictionary* has a foreign language counterpart, and *Children of The Americas* is a very readable and gayly illustrated series of books for children from five to eight. Use a foreign dictionary to help you with words you don't know:

To keep the family interest on a high level, you might, by a number of clever ways, add incentive. For example, you might try making foreign word cards for furniture and household articles and hanging a card on each piece of equipment. This helps children recognize words in relationship to articles. Or you might try writing mysterious messages on cards in your new language. Whoever reads and translates this message finds a small surprise or treat such as a candy bar or gum. You can have a treasure hunt with the clues written in French, Italian, or Spanish. You add spice and variety by having a meal each week where only your new language is spoken and penalties can be made if English is spoken. Of course a good part of the meal will probably be eaten in silence or with sign language, but this too might be an advantage!

14.

Fit for Fun

The health of the nation is one of the major concerns of every President of the United States. Various "Youth Fitness" programs have been instigated with emphasis on improving the physical fitness of the people. These programs are worthy ones and the family can surely do much to cooperate. Physical well-being doesn't necessarily mean that Dad must be out on the golf course every Saturday and Sunday, while Mom goes bowling with her league to keep in trim. Physical fitness can be a family project with Mom, Dad, and the children all joining in. By planning family activities which are healthful and which everyone enjoys, you can attain not only physical fitness, but a closer knit family. There are countless activities that meet these requirements.

For example, how about an evening of rough-housing? "Horrors," you say. "The neighbors will think mayhem is taking place." Actually, rough-housing is more than fun. It's great exercise, using nearly every muscle in the body. If some of the family shy away from this activity, how about trying an old-fashioned pillow fight? Maybe a little hard on the pillows but it's great fun for the kids!

Simple gymnastics are lots of fun to do and they strengthen every muscle. You can do simple rollovers, handstands, wheelbarrow walks, spider walks, and head-stands or tugs-of-war on your living room floor or on your back lawn. If you don't know much about these exercises and drills, the Boy Scout Handbook on Physical Fitness or a book from your library will suggest gymnastics you can introduce easily. We have salvaged several old cushions and mattresses from cast-off furniture and covered them with sturdy denim slip covers. These make wonderful gym pads when spread on the floor or the grass. They make ideal tumbling pads for pyramid building, wrestling, and a dozen other exercises. The denim covers are easily washed and stay bright and sturdy.

Another family project combining fun and fitness is bicycling. There are places a family can get on bicycles that a car can never take them, and the dividends in fun alone make it worthwhile. You may want to take a lunch along and stop by a lovely grove or a brook for refreshment and rest. A "Nose-bag" lunch or a hobo knapsack can be carried by each member of the party.

Probably the best all-around conditioner is swimming. Most families have access to a beach or swimming pool during the summer months and it's lots of fun to get the family together for a game of water polo or tag. Swimming races, with a handicap depending on swimming ability, are fun. A relay race against the family next door at the end of the season would be an incentive to train.

Horseback riding is another activity high on the list of fun sports that help build strong bodies. Some Saturday try renting or borrowing horses for the whole family to ride and see how delightful this exercise can be. You may be stiff and sore if it is your first ride, but once you learn to ride properly, you'll develop most of the right muscles.

All of the group participation sports are fun and good conditioners too. You'll want to try volley ball, badminton, tennis, and touch football. The whole family, as well as the neighbors, can play these games. Even the so-called "children's games" can be fun for families. There's no loss of dignity in playing "Here Come Some Jolly Butcher Boys," "Run, Sheep, Run," "Beckon," or "Kick the Can." Parents are to be applauded when they join in such active fun games on family night.

Camping—Hiking

Camping is a wonderful activity for families, especially if you go off where you have to rough it a bit. There is much merit in taking your family out on a rugged camping trip far from the busy urban centers where nature is either distorted or obliterated altogether. We don't mean camping in a modern trailer camp with all the convenience of home. We mean real honest-to-goodness outdoor camping where survival depends on your own efforts and resourcefulness. Families who venture into this type of camping recommend it with overwhelming approval and enthusiasm. They feel that the family becomes a little more self-sufficient, more reliable, more appreciative of nature, and a little more physically fit when it comes in close contact with the great unspoiled outdoors.

There are many places in our country which offer rugged adventure in outdoor living. There is a national park within easy driving distance of almost every area in America. If you haven't toured the national parks near your home, plan on doing so with your children at your next opportunity. These exhilarating areas dot our country and offer everything from burro trips through Glacier National Park to studies of the Pueblo dwellers at Mesa Verde.

Hiking and camping trips can be found anyplace you want to pitch your tent and start out. None are as extensive as the Appalachian Trail, 2,000 miles of marked path, but many beautiful trails are found in natural country. The largest community hike in the world is the annual Timpanogos hike, which attracts several thousand hikers to Provo, Utah, each July. This 14-mile hike past glaciers and waterfalls of unsurpassed beauty is well worth the climb. The panoramic view from the top of Mt. Timp is breathtakingly beautiful. The beautiful White Mountain National Forest is a mecca for mountain climbers and offers over a thousand miles of trails.

For some families, great joy can be found in sharing a week's camping vacation with other families. After a week of sharing experiences, exploring the surrounding country together and worshiping together, the joy of being together as families, not separated into age groups, is greatly deepened. Evenings spent around the campfire telling tall tales and singing favorite songs is an experience parents and children will never forget.

For those families who love water, there are marvelous boating trips in the Wisconsin lake region, the Upper Colorado in Southern Utah, the Ozarks and the Mississippi River. Many of our beautiful bodies of water, such as the Great Lakes and St. Lawrence Seaway offer boat trips, as do the many coastal islands on the Eastern, Western and Gulf shores.

If you live near a body of water, river, or stream, and are looking for a sport that is relaxing, exciting, adventuresome and not too strenuous, then you'll love "tubing." Just gather up your inflated inner tubes and try floating down the river some summer afternoon, seated firmly in the innertube. This can become a favorite family pastime. The only equipment needed is an inflated innertube for each one and a sense of fun and adventure. This is much more exciting than just floating along in a boat because in a tube you bob along with every rise in the water and bounce with the current. If you get out of the current, it takes some frantic paddling with your hands to get back in. But it can be lots of fun. Bathing suits or old shorts are the standard costume in our area.

Tubing is not a sport for small children. We have a rule that everyone on the river must know how to swim, or have passed their swimming merit badge. If you want to take younger ones along, insist on life jackets, and lash their innertubes to an adult's with a strong rope.

Walking

A noted writer and statesman, speaking about the jet age, made the comment that people are thrilled to circle the whole earth in a few minutes, but they won't spend even five minutes walking in the woods. And yet, if they are perceptive and discerning they would learn more about God and His creations in the woods than they will on a jet flight. It is where you find sweet violets hidden in a wood bank, or the nest of wild birds, that you will discover much of the beauties of the world. Do not handicap your children by piling them in the family automobile to go as fast and far as possible on every family holiday. If you do, they will miss much because the choicest places will not exist for them. These places can't be seen from the family car.

It's true you can drive along *some* highways where the wild apple blossoms or the dogwood are in bloom. But you will miss much of the gentle unfolding of spring as you speed by. Instead, why don't you take time to stop and pick up "treasures" of interesting rocks, colorful bird feathers, or to look for a fairy glen! If you know what to look for, you can't miss!

We didn't discover the joy of walking as a family until some good friends and neighbors returned from a three year stay in Germany. While there, their five children had all become accustomed to the delightful pastime of *walking*. The first Sunday after their return the children invited our children to go for a walk with them. When they returned, much later, we found they had walked over two miles and our children had loved every minute of it. They hadn't even minded the spring shower that overtook them on the way! Since then, each season finds us walking. In the fall we take an exhilarating walk through heaps of crunchy leaves; in the winter there is the satisfying crunch of snow underfoot, crisp and cold; in the summer we look for wild berries along the way.

Our boys, both Scouts, have practiced laying an Indian trail and using a compass to keep us heading in the right direction. They easily imagine they are tracking Indians or exploring as frontier scouts.

Even if you live in the city, don't deprive your child of the joy of "exploring" or walking. There are many fascinating things to be seen if you but take time to be observant and find joy in little things as seen through the eyes of a child. It's fun to watch the construction of a new office building, to look in the window of a pet store, to window-shop at the five and dime, to see the lovely window displays, to enjoy the glitter of the bright lights at night. All these things and many others can be enjoyed in a leisurely walk, but not from a speeding car!

HIPPETY HIPPETY HIP HURRAY
SATURDAY WILL BE CIRCUS DAY!

15.

Have a Circus!

WHAT CHILD HAS KNOWN REAL EXCITEMENT UNTIL HE HAS seen a circus, or better still, been *in* a circus? Just think what glad anticipation this announcement brings to those who hear it, young and old.

Though it's a long way from the huge colosseum of ancient Rome (where the first circus took place as early as 61 B.C.) to the pleasant dew and dust-smelling familiarity of your own back yard, still the color, clamor, and confusion of the circus, *any circus*, remain the same. Whether there are 400,000 spectators in the Circus Maximus watching chariot races, games, and wild animal acts or the neighborhood moms applauding the tremulous hand stands, faltering recitations, and harum-scarum performances of their own "troupers," the circus is still "the greatest show on earth."

Here are the irresistible "come-ons" of the barker, and the blaring, brassy music of the circus band! Here are the colorful balloons and bright flags; the gaudily painted signs proclaiming the wonders of the world (and who's to say that they are not?), the gay costumes of every size, shape, and color, from the fragile pastel ballerina to the blatant, noisy clowns.

And you can be part of all of it—you and your family, neighbors, and community. There is nothing like a circus to cure summer doldrums, to stimulate interest in a group project, to help a family find companionship together, or to raise funds for a worthy cause. Children bored? Plan a circus! Family at swords' points? Try a circus! Neighborhood at loose end? Have a circus! Building a new church? Need money for the Scouts? Then by all means have a circus! For any reason or for no reason at all, have a circus!

Just think what fun it is to see a performance under the Big Top. Then think how exciting it is to *take part* in such a performance. You'll find rich rewards, moneywise or otherwise, if you but follow these suggestions for organizing and producing a circus that will be remembered long after the sawdust has settled and the pleas for more lipstick, pins, and lemonade have abated.

Getting *ready* for the performance is almost as much fun as the actual production itself—and just how extensive the preparation will depend on why and where you are having the circus. Obviously if it's in your own back yard for the benefit of your family and close neighbors, the beforehand work necessary won't be as much as if you were planning a money-making circus for a cub pack or church group. The latter will entail publicity and involve many more committees and assignments.

Actually an amateur circus can be put on any time of year—the only difference is where it will be staged. Usually summer and warm weather put us in the mood for an outdoor event and surely ice-cold lemonade and popcorn are deliciously refreshing on a hot summer day. But in the colder months or inclement weather it will be necessary to move into a basement recreation room, a gymnasium, or even an auditorium.

If you are planning a back-yard circus in your own or a neighboring yard, you will want to look over the setting several days before the big event. Keep an eye open for the best possibility for setting up the midway, the performers' "ring," the menagerie, the main entrance, *and* the audience.

If the performance attracts a large crowd, it is helpful to hold it in a place where seats are available for the audience. But even if they are not, don't let this deter you. Folding chairs, benches (real or improvised from planks and up-ended boxes), stools, or just a lawn itself can be used. Even blankets and throw rugs will be more than adequate, for who's thinking of comfort when such a brilliant star-spangled spectacle is taking place?

If a more extensive program than a simple neighborhood gathering is planned, a park, ball field, or playground will be necessary. If the park or yard has a slight grade, so much the better for it will provide a natural amphitheater for your production. If the circus is for a large crowd such as a YMCA group or cub pack, then you may want to have a committee construct a simple stage with curtains, backdrops, and screens for the performers to dress behind. If your stage has no curtains, improvise them by holding up blankets. Of course, if it's a back-yard circus, a clothesline makes a wonderful curtain prop with sheets or blankets hung by safety pins so that they slide easily along the line.

The word gets around mighty fast that important things are going on when a back-yard circus is planned, and you will have no trouble recruiting volunteers to help! You'll be swamped with genuine offers to help hang pennants and flags, to sack popcorn, blow balloons, paint circus posters, and to do all the enticing jobs that go into putting on a "big top" performance. However, in organizing a circus—either large or small—someone obviously must be in charge. A responsible mother or dad in the neighborhood may be sympathetic to the idea and give the enthusiastic time and support necessary to get the show on the road. With very little incentive the children will rally round, eager as beavers to help in every way.

However, if the circus is planned on a large scale, some advance work will be necessary. A general chairman such as a cubmaster or committee man will need to be in charge of coordinating all the activities and preparations. Sub-committees will need to be assigned to take care of arranging for physical facilities (the park, ball field, or building where the circus will be held, and the seating arrangements), publicity and advertising, record player and public address system, tickets, refreshments, decorations (signs, posters, flags, and carnival trappings), the circus performance (acts and stunts), midway games and concessions, and prizes. You may also want a prompter and sound-effects man. For a really amateur circus a rehearsal is not necessary. By reading through the rest of this book and selecting those acts and games that will fit in well with your situation, you can plan a reasonably carefree show featuring many of the attractions of a more ambitious production.

For a family or neighborhood affair, you will not need advertising posters or publicity announcements. The grapevine will suffice! However, you may wish to issue verbal invitations to the other families included. Or better still, add to the color and excitement of the enterprise by making invitations to send out. A number of suggestions follow:

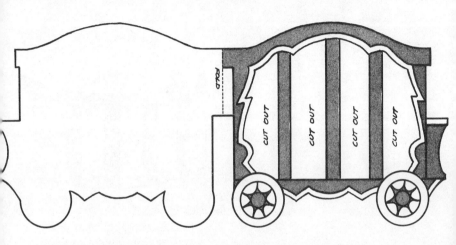

Trace and cut out, using yellow construction paper. Cut out the spaces between the bars. Fold so that back matches front, and paste four corners and bottom, leaving space at the top so that the lion can be put into the circus wagon. Add a splash of red paint or crayon around the edge of the cage opening.

These lines appear inside the front cover:
>Hurry, Hurry, Hurry
>To the Greatest Show on Earth!

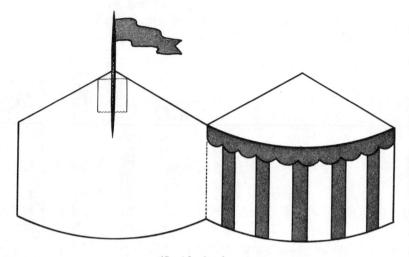

(Inside back cover)
>Come one, come all,
>See our giraffe so tall,
>See our elephant walk,
>Hear our monkey talk.
>The circus is in town,
>We have a funny clown.
>Next Tuesday at 4:00 P.M.,
>This ticket will let you in.
>135 East 2nd North   Paxmans

This happy elephant can be used as an invitation or, where tables are used, as a placecard. Use construction paper or cardboard. Write invitation verse on back.

This simple invitation uses a 3″ x 5″ file card. Paste bright round construction paper cutouts on the card to represent balloons or color the circles.

Please come to our
Gigantic Circus
Friday, September 3
5 p.m.
123 White Street
Admission 35¢
Invite all your friends!
Free Popcorn, Treats, Balloons, Games, Prizes!

The following verse can be substituted:
> Hippity, Hippity, Hip-Hooray!
> Next Saturday will be circus day.
> The posters say there'll be three rings
> And lovely ladies in high-rope swings.
> There'll be many clowns in their funny hats,
> Trained seals, and monkeys, and acrobats.
> Please be here promptly at the "Big Top"
> For a barrel of fun and a bottle of pop.
> Hippity, Hippity, Hip-Hooray!
> Next Saturday will be circus day.
> 2:00 P.M.   Paxmans   Saturday, July____
> Back yard 135 East 2nd North

This happy clown has a small balloon inserted for a nose and yellow yarn inserted at the lower edge of his cap for hair. A yarn tassle to top his cap can be added.

If you are looking for a quick way to cover the neighborhood, send out home dittoed or mimeographed notices such as this little bulletin. Here again volunteers can be recruited to cover a lot of territory in a hurry. Be sure your notices stipulate the time, place, and admission price if there is to be one. Make the lettering as neat as possible.

**11th Annual
NEIGHBORHOOD**

CIRCUS!

**WEDNESDAY AUG. 12th 4 pm
135 E. 2nd No. PROVO**

BENEFIT: PRIMARY CHILDREN'S HOSPITAL

**25¢ INCLUDES : ADMISSION,
REFRESHMENTS, GAMES,
MERRY-GO-ROUND, MIDWAY
FUN, ETC., ETC.**

If the circus is to be a real money-making project, you will want to advertise more extensively. The local newspapers will be an asset if you submit stories and photographs telling in a colorful way the details of the project and its worthy purpose. You will also want to make and display attractive posters announcing and advertising

your show. These can be original or traced from coloring books using show card, cardboard, or butcher paper as background. The lettering can be done with poster paints, crayons, colored chalk, or water colors; felt-tipped pens are ideal for lettering and come in a variety of colors. Here again be sure to give the time, place, date, and price.

If your aim is to raise money for a worthwhile project such as the Children's Hospital, Cub Scouts, PTA, Church Building Fund, or 4-H group, there are several ways to proceed. You can charge an over-all general admission that will cover everything including refreshments and games; you can charge a small admission fee and then make a slight charge for participation in each game on the midway and for refreshments; you can provide the main show and midway free and charge only for refreshments which are sold from gaily-decorated booths. The committee can decide the amount to charge and the method to be used.

If your money-raising project is a valid one, you may be able to persuade civic-minded merchants to donate prizes and refreshments, thus increasing your profits considerably. Many firms will donate balloons used in advertising in addition to pencils, comic books, novelties, whistles, and other stock items that will be useful in a fish pond or as prizes for games. Grocery stores will often help out by contributing cartons of gum or candy bars. And local soft drink or ice-cream distributors may be willing to furnish your refreshments in return for advertising and good will. If local businessmen do contribute to your circus, be sure to mention their generosity during the circus performance. You may wish to display a sign listing the names of cooperating merchants.

Refreshments

The very mention of a circus naturally brings to mind refreshments for what's a circus without popcorn, peanuts, and pink lemonade. Barkers with colorful baskets of candy and crackerjack, bright-colored punch and animal crackers may act as vendors and peddle their tempting goodies between acts. Or a refreshment booth may handle this trade. A soda-pop stand is especially welcome in the summer time. If the circus is a group project such as for a cub scout pack, then assign one den to pop and bag the popcorn, one to furnish paper cups and pink lemonade (the frozen variety is very inexpensive and quite delicious), one to bring home-made candy, and another the animal crackers thus dividing up the responsibility.

Decorations and Displays

Your own happy memories of childhood circus thrills will be a guide to the decorations needed. Naturally you'll think of bright signs and costumes, gay banners waving from the tops of high poles, flags of all sizes, and quaint posters depicting fierce animals, trainers, and side-show oddities.

The following illustrations might be useful in stimulating your imagination. You may wish to choose a few of the ideas and then add to your collection if your circus becomes an annual event.

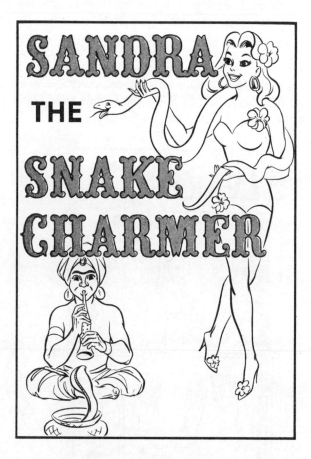

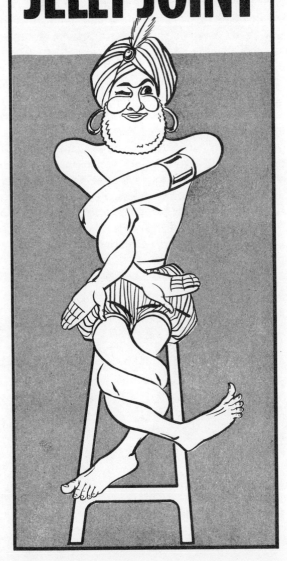

Large panels of cardboard such as those found in appliance or mattress packing cases are ideal for signs, and your local dealer will save them for you if you ask him. Show-card paper, butcher paper, or even newsprint salvage from the newspaper plant can also be used as a background for signs.

Lacking a "big top," a simulated canvas can be achieved by using long strips of paper 12–15 inches wide and painting vertical stripes every 3 or 4 inches. The paper can be scalloped and then tacked up along the walls or eaves of the house or garage. Luminous paint makes the colors stand out vividly though it is more expensive than regular paint. Gaily decorated booths will supply plenty of color and attractive background. Use card tables or kitchen tables and make a framework by tacking 2" upright boards into the ground in front of the table. Brace the top and cover with a canopy of bright crêpe paper, oilcloth, bunting, or striped butcher paper.

Designate the main entrance with a sign made from a large cardboard carton panel such as refrigerators come in. Paint in big bright red letters "Main Entrance," and edge the sign with colorful, crinkled crêpe paper of contrasting colors. Place the sign over the entrance way or across the door frame if the circus is held indoors. Outside it can be supported by bamboo poles or 1" x 2" lumber strips. Make the sign and uprights secure by attaching wires from the top of the sign to the nearest tree or house. Use whatever space is available

on the supporting wires to pin or staple crêpe paper streamers. Huge side-show posters which can be placed at the sides of the Main Entrance sign can be painted on the large panels of paper in which mattresses come wrapped or on the cardboard from the mattress carton. The heavy paper panels have the advantage of being more easily folded for storage. The illustration will give you some ideas for drawing your sign.

Near the main entrance you will also want to set up a ticket booth where tickets may be sold, an admission fee paid, or tickets given out for the concessions and refreshments. Old packing cases which have been used for transporting refrigerators make ideal ticket booths. Simply knock out both ends and the back and provide a low platform for the ticket seller. A single board nailed across the center of the case provides a shelf on which to make change. Paint the box in bright colors. The "barker" in charge of the ticket booth can be dressed in a loud, bright-colored shirt or vest (just cut out and sew a bright piece of material to the front of a regular vest) and a derby hat (purchased from a costume house or novelty shop). A mustache

and sideburns can be painted on him. A "spiel," as the barker's chant is called, can be found on page 135. Additional ticket sellers may assist the barker by proclaiming their spiels from nearby booths or while mingling with the crowd. Unless you have selected as barkers very aggressive and competent people who can think quickly and improvise humorously, it would be better to have them memorize their lines so that their delivery will be good. Of course if the children are doing this on their own, they will prove to be quite resourceful and will not need to memorize their "come-ons."

Strip tickets can be made by marking strips of paper into sections with a pencil. Next stitch these pencilled sections on your sewing machine (having first removed the thread and bobbin) and they will then be perforated just like real tickets. You may want to charge 25¢ (or more) for a strip of tickets.

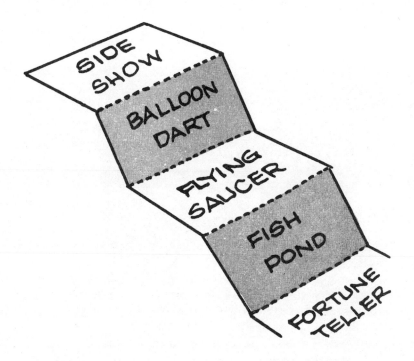

If the circus is held indoors, a ticket table can be set up by the door or a regular box office may be used if one is available.

Large grocery stores or other chain stores often use a circus theme in their advertising programs. When their promotional program is over they will usually be glad to give you their signs, posters, and other paraphernalia if you ask for them. If you see such a display, arrange with the manager to have the materials saved for you. We are sure that many store managers will be more than willing to cooperate if they are approached with courtesy and consideration. Several years ago when we were traveling through a distant state, we stopped at a large grocery store where a circus theme was being used. We asked the manager if he would save the materials for us when he was finished with them. Leaving a large self-addressed manila envelope and adequate postage to cover cost of mailing, we returned to our home. Several weeks later we were delighted to receive all the materials used in the store. The two-foot-high luminous letters spelling out "The Greatest Show on Earth" have been fastened with masking tape to the wall of our brick barn and the many animal posters have also been used effectively.

Cagey Capers

What's a circus without a menagerie? Set aside some area where all the toys and stuffed animals can be displayed and hang a large sign over the area which says "Menagerie" or "Cagey Capers." Have the children scour the neighborhood for all the ferocious lions, tigers, elephants, monkeys, bears, dogs, and squirrels they can find. To house them you must have cages, of course, so contact the produce department of your local grocery and have them save orange crates or produce crates such as lettuce comes in. Decorate the "cages" by winding brightly-colored crêpe paper around the slats. Place the crates upside down on card tables, and identify each wild animal with a small printed sign. As an alternative, you may wish to display all kinds of live household pets—baby turtles, dogs, cats, birds, white mice, parakeets, guinea pigs, and so on. Cages can also be made from wooden boxes with decorative tops cut from plywood and painted in bright circus colors. Use dowel sticks as bars to confine the ferocious animals. A more elaborate circus wagon cage can be made by using a child's wagon as a base and building wooden or cardboard box bars to fit on top. This cage could house a pet dog or a child dressed in an animal costume. Put straw on the floor of the cage and provide a bucket for the child to sit on. You may want to assign each participating family or den to the responsibility of constructing one of these circus wagons.

If you have back-yard swings available, post a "Trapeze" sign on them. If you are fortunate enough to have a teeter-totter that re-volves, you can label it "Merry-Go-Round" or "Carousel."

In some areas, certain business firms have on a trailer a small six to eight horse merry-go-round which is operated electrically and can be transported easily. This you might be able to borrow or rent inex-pensively if your circus is a money-making proposition for a worth-while charity. In our area, the Continental Baking Company has been most generous in furnishing their small merry-go-round for our Children's Hospital benefit circus.

Every circus, indoors or out, must have a tall circus pole in the center of the ring! This can be made from long cardboard tubes ob-tained from your local carpet or linoleum dealers. Place the tubes over a sturdy pole such as a tether ball pole, or support them with three or four wires fastened in a secure place. The wires can be used to hold colored pennants made from plastic, crêpe paper, or inexpensive cloth. These are usually cut in triangular shapes and they can be pinned or stapled over the wire. To the top of the cardboard tube fly a 4- to 6-foot triangular pennant.

Another attractive decoration can be made using hula hoops. Cover each hula hoop with white butcher paper and fasten the paper to the hoop with masking tape or paste. Cut an "X" in the center of the paper just large enough so that a toy animal's head and fore feet can protrude. Secure the rest of the body to the back of the hoop with thin wire so it stays in place. Hang the animal hoops on the walls or in strategic places.

Your midway for games and concessions will be another area where gay decorations and bright signs will promote a circus atmosphere. A good place to set the games up would be on a paved driveway, a tennis court, or around the outside edges of a lawn. It is important to leave the center area free for the performances in the "ring"

so that the spectators can sit comfortably on chairs, benches, blankets, or on the grass itself. Detailed description of the midway and the games to be played can be found on pages 176–187.

The stage for the performance can be the lawn, a wide porch or patio area, or a temporary platform. Clotheslines make excellent curtain rods and can serve as backdrops when covered with sheets, blankets, or painted scenery. Large cardboard posters can be used to fill in the additional space, providing a closed-off area from which performers can make their exits and entrances. Clowns, other performers, or the ringmaster can either open and close the curtains between acts or the performers can simply step through the curtain opening to perform in front of the curtains.

Circuses are full of all kinds of music from calliope to blaring bands and there are many excellent records available. Use this lively circus music with the blaring trombones and trumpets and spirited roll of the drums playing in the background to help provide the authentic circus atmosphere. "Circus Time" (Decca DL8451) and "Circus Band" (Capitol 265) are both recorded by the Ringling Bros. and Barnum and Bailey and with Merle Evans conducting. These records include special music for the parade, acrobats, wild animals, clowns, and other performers. "Nickelodean and Calliope" (Cook 10350) features authentic calliope music, and for the side show numbers you might like "Carousel" (Cook 10120) or "Sounds of Carnival" (Folkways FPX126) which is full of midway sounds and music. Use these records as background music from the time the first guest arrives until the performance actually begins. Then the thrilling music can also fill in any slack between acts.

If you want to construct your own calliope, obtain a boy's wagon for a base and use various sizes of cardboard tubes painted gold to represent the pipes. Install a record player inside.

If you prefer to use live music, let a group of children dressed in clown suits or band uniforms play their instruments. A band wagon can be made by using a wagon with a flat top which has benches attached to it. A cub scout den or neighborhood group could be given such an assignment. Other musical numbers could be provided by a "bottle band"—a group of musicians who play tunes on bottles filled with varying amounts of water "tuned" to a certain pitch. Cigar-box banjoes, paper and comb combinations, a harmonica band, or a "kitchen" orchestra (instruments made from various utensils) could all be used to furnish musical numbers. Of course, you will want to feature any bona fide musicians you may have, either as entreé acts or as part of the main show itself.

A public address system will boost the volume to pandemonium and delight the kids as well as the adults. A public address system is indispensable if the circus is held outdoors or if the crowd is large; it will amplify the recorded music, the ringmaster's announcements, and the performers' sounds.

Costumes

Almost everyone, certainly *every* child—loves to be in a circus, so if your circus is an informal affair, suggest on your invitation that each child wear some costume suitable to a circus act. Even if they don't perform, they'll feel part of the act if they are dressed up. These costumes need not be a problem for anyone. They can be borrowed, begged, or improvised and they need not be elaborate or expensive.

Most mothers can salvage dancing costumes, band uniforms, and pageant, operetta, or school-play costumes to dress their youngsters in. Brother's Boy Scout trousers coupled with Mother's riding boots make a fine ringmaster's outfit. Imagination will do wonders with prosaic everyday materials from sewing baskets or discarded clothing. Many props for clown suits can be found by rummaging through the attic. (Clown costumes as such are discussed on page 136.)

Some very inexpensive circus costumes such as clown hats can be made from paper sacks. Choose a sack that fits the head. Cut along open end; fold top to a point and pin or staple. If you like, paint the hat in bright colors and pin small cotton balls to it. To make a clown mask use the part of the sack cut away. Cut holes for eyes. Draw features. Fasten strings for ties. To make a ruffle, sew crêpe paper through the middle with a strong thread and gather. Leave long ends of string for tying.

A paper bag can also be made into an animal trainer's hat. Cut the sack in two. Color the hat and attach a visor as illustrated. Tie a shoelace to a long stick to make a trainer's whip.

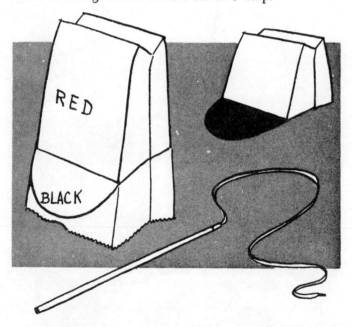

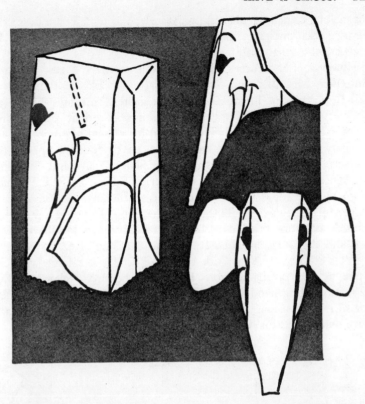

To make an elephant mask from a paper sack, use a large bag and be sure it fits the head. Cut out each side as illustrated and cut holes for the eyes. Use the rest of the bag for ears which are attached with glue or staples.

Other animal costumes can also be made from larger bags or large pieces of wrapping paper. Cut out animal heads using the fold at the top. Staple the sides together and lightly stuff the head with paper to give it shape. Two-piece carnival costumes can be made the same way. Cut out the body with the fold at the top of the back and fasten the head and a tail to the body with staples. One child then wears the head and another the body. Paint the paper animals so that they resemble real animals, giving your leopard brown spots, your zebra black and white stripes, and so forth. See the illustration for making camels, elephants, ponies, cats, and pigs. These heads can be used with one-piece suits, such as sleepers or long underwear, for one-person animal costumes.

However, if it is necessary or desirable to make a new costume, Butterick, McCall's, and Simplicity pattern books contain quite a variety of patterns for animal and fancy dress costumes which can be inexpensively made from cotton prints or bright plain-colored percale. Suede or outing flannel is good for animal costumes.

Many excellent costume suggestions can be found in pamphlets such as: "How to Make Costumes for School Plays and Pageants" by Agnes Lilley, published by the Service Bureau of RIT Products Corporation, 1437 West Morris Street, Indianapolis 6, Indiana; "Colorful Costumes" published by Dennison, Dept. 517, Framingham, Massachusetts (25¢); "Inexpensive Costumes for Plays, Festivals and Pageants" by Nina R. Lamkin, National. Rec. Association, 8 West 8th Street, New York 11, N. Y. (25¢). A catalog with costume helps is available from Recreation Service, Delaware, Ohio (25¢). Scouting handbooks and quarterlies are full of costume ideas for various occasions and children's coloring and cutout books also have many ideas for costumes.

You will want to assemble a properties box that will include old hats, dresses, coats, umbrellas, flowers, canes, loud ties, wigs, beads, feathers, gloves, bright scarves, sashes, dressing gowns, shoes, Halloween costumes and masks, pajamas, trousers, robes, kimonas, rag mops for wigs and beards, veils, sandals, thongs, and moccasins. Oilcloth and lamés, lace curtains, old draperies, and burlap sacking can be used for special effects.

Also a make-up box including powder, lipstick, eyebrow pencil, and grease paint will come in handy. A little lipstick and rouge will be sufficient for the lady acrobats, bareback riders, and dancers. Clowns can use colorful grease paint to exaggerate their eyes, nose, and mouth. Indians and darker-skinned performers should use dark powders. Eyebrow pencils and liners are useful in shaping oriental features.

The specific costumes for each suggested performer are included in the description of the act and are listed under the respective names.

The Circus

And now the big moment has arrived. The circus is ready to start.

The band begins to play, the first guests arrive, and the Barker in derby hat, brightly colored vest, and flowing mustache hurries everyone in as he calls with a staccato voice:

"Hurry, hurry, hurry; step right up ladies and gentlemen and purchase your tickets for the main show! The Big Show! Here you have it. The big show of the afternoon. This is what you came to see and the show is about to begin. Step right up, step right up, and I'll tell you what you're going to see! You'll see daring damsels risking their dainty necks as they bravely walk the tight wire. You'll see the fiercest of wild animals from every corner and cave on this earth. And this isn't all you'll see inside the big show. Ladies and gentlemen get your tickets now. Step right up folks. Don't push, don't crowd! You'll see the Wild Man from Borneo. You'll see beautiful bareback riders. The show is about to begin. Get your tickets; get your tickets now for the big event. You'll see Dapper Dan, the lion tamer. Man, you say it's not enough, you want more? All right, I'll tell you what I'm going to do. Without any additional cost to you whatsoever, I'm going to give you coupons that will entitle you to refreshments of the highest delectibility, and if you're a holder of a lucky ticket, you'll get balloons and prizes and entertainment galore. Now step right up folks. Purchase your tickets for 25¢, just a quarter part of a dollar, and take your seat for the main event. You'll be entertained until the performance starts by the world famous circus band, an aggregation of the most famous musicians gathered for your pleasure from the great conservatories of music throughout the world. All right folks, step right up, get your tickets, come in and see the big show. This is something you can't afford to miss. The clowns are now performing and the main show will soon begin. So get your tickets now. Step right up, hurry, hurry, hurry. Here you have it. From every corner of the globe we have assembled wondrous personages for your entertainment. Get your tickets now. Only 25¢, a quarter of a dollar! A quarter, a quarter. Step right up and get your tickets for this glittering performance. There's something for everyone. Hurry, Hurry, Hurry. Get your popcorn, peanuts, and soda pop on the way in. The show is about to begin. Step right up and get your tickets!" Parts of the spiel are repeated as new arrivals appear on the scene.

While the audience is assembling, you will want to have the circus band playing background music while the clowns perform novelty stunts. Guests may inspect the menageries and observe the animals in their cages. If this is a fund-raising event, you may want to open the midway games and concessions before the main show. Participants can also enjoy the sideshow attractions, freak booths, skill games, fortune telling, refreshment stands, and the fish pond while they are awaiting the big-ring performance.

As soon as the crowd has assembled and been seated around the area selected as the big ring or main arena, the Grand Parade begins. The ringmaster is dressed in riding boots (or black oilcloth leggings), breeches (white if available), shirt, top hat and flowing cape (a band uniform cape or nurse's cape). He announces the show and keeps everything moving from the opening parade and the "Star Spangled Banner" to the glittering finale. He announces the color guard that leads the parade. Usually a Scout Troop or Cub Den will provide boys for this ceremony and they carry the American flag and other flags or banners. They lead the audience in the Pledge of Allegiance or the "Star Spangled Banner" and then the parade begins—and what a parade! Everyone is in it! Freaks, clowns, side-

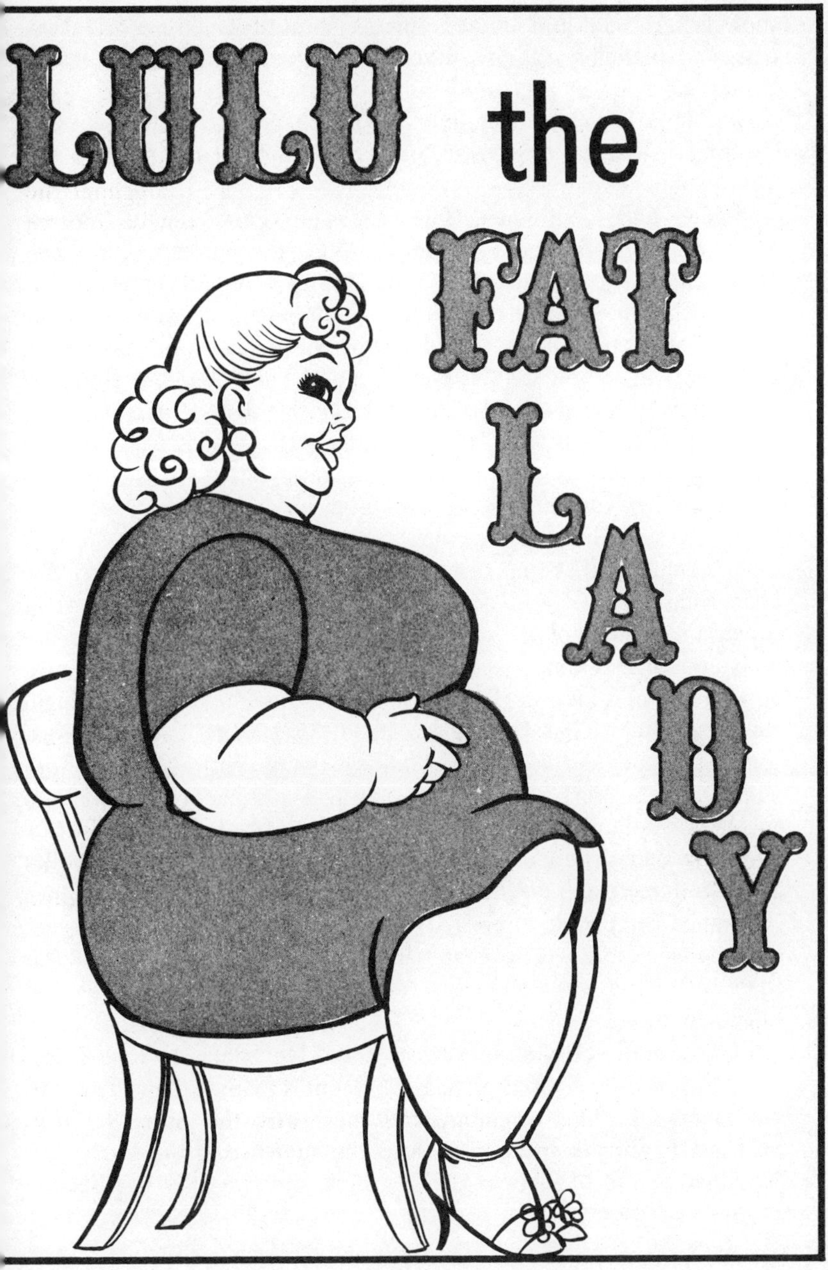
LULU the FAT LADY

show artists, wild and trained animals, beautiful dancers and acrobats, and prancing stallions. Even the wagons with red and yellow barred cages are in the parade to add a realistic touch. The record player blares forth a spirited march as all the performers wind around the arena while the ringmaster, using a megaphone or amplifier says in an eloquent manner:

"Ladies and Gentlemen, The Circus on Parade! The Greatest Show on Earth is about to begin. We (the Primary Children's Hospital or Monument Park Cub Scouts) proudly present the Grand Entrance Parade! Ladies and Gentlemen, please arise as the flag comes by and join in the Pledge of Allegiance. And now Ladies and Gentlemen, you see the great array of talent brought from the far corners of the globe for your entertainment and pleasure. First comes the Parade of the Nations, representatives from many distant lands wearing the colorful national costumes. They are led by Miss Liberty. Now you see the clowns followed by Sandra, the Snake Charmer, and Herman Hercules, the strongest man in the world. Give them a hand as they come by! Folks, now see the Fat Lady, the bedazzling Bareback Riders, and the Hula Dancers, brought at great expense from the golden sands of Waikiki! And now the Wild Animals and their Trainer. Here's Jojo the juggler, the Bearded Lady, and Eddy, the Educated Horse. Just look at those high-prancing, high-stepping ponies! Give them a big hand! Here's the Tattooed Man, the Tightrope Walkers, the Monkey doing acrobatics, and the Trained Seals. Next we have our Magician and the Tallest Man in the World followed by the Midgets and the Gypsy Fortune Teller. And now come the Cowboys and Indians! They're all here! Ladies and Gentlemen, let's give them a big hand!"

Arrange the parade any way you want, but keep it moving along by spacing performers so that while each can be adequately seen, there will be no long empty spaces between performers. A suggested lineup follows:

Color Guard—carrying massed flags and banners.

Parade of the Nations—led by Miss Liberty or Uncle Sam followed by guests dressed in colorful costumes such as Irish, Dutch, Italian, Hungarian, South American, and so on.

Comedy Cops or Clowns

Snake Charmers

Bareback Riders
Siamese Twins
Goop Clowns
Wild Animals and Trainer—animals in wagon cages, or sulking
    along ahead of trainer's cracking whip.
Clown Tramps
Strong Man
Bearded Lady
Jojo the Juggler
Fat Lady
Educated Horse
Tallest Man in the World
Minstrel Quartet
Seals
Tattooed Man—wearing bathrobe or dressing gown
Tightrope Walkers—carrying parasols
Clowns
Monkey and Trainer
Ballet Dancers
Magician
Fortune Teller
Wild Man
Midget
Trick Shooters
Cowboys and Indians

After circling the ring once or twice, the performers exit to the assembly area where they wait until called upon to do their act.

The circus acts are now introduced with a dazzling and eloquent build-up by the ringmaster. Most children will want very much to get into the act though they will probably be reluctant to do much practicing beforehand. An encouraging adult or a smooth-talking youngster can ad-lib as the announcer and talk most youngsters through their performances. Actually most of the acts for an informal neighborhood circus can be done with little or no rehearsal at all though some such as the magician, minstrel quartet, and dancers will have to practice in order to put on a convincing performance. Most children are actors par excellence and with a few instructions can readily fit into a make-believe role with surprising alacrity. Some of the sweetest and most satisfying facial expressions will be seen when the children appear briefly in one of the suggested circus acts.

Intersperse musical numbers with dramatic acts or pageantry and arrange to have simple stunts or clown antics between the acts.

Since the clowns make up a goodly portion of any circus, we'll discuss clowns' costumes, make-up, and stunts first. Clowns can play many roles in many ways throughout the entire production; they can substitute for property men and stage hands and refreshment vendors as well as provide comic relief.

Broad slapstick comedy goes over big with a circus audience if it is kept moving at a swift pace and doesn't lapse into humorless gesturing. The clowns can put on a special production number which involves preparation and is done as a rehearsed or at least a well-planned act or they can be merely used as interludes or incidents between featured performances. Numerous skit and stunt books such as those published by the Boy Scouts of America, available at the local scout office, or *Skits and Stunts* published by the National Recreation Association, will give you numerous ideas for clever clown acts.

Many clever boys and girls will enjoy working out their own interlude or simple incident act, usually called a "walk around" in the circus trade. Outlandish and incongruous costumes salvaged from the attic or from rummage sales are wonderful for this type of stunt. For example, an old fur coat and a fan are incongruous enough to provoke laughter. Or a ski suit and fishing pole or golf clubs will arouse guffaws. A number of clowns may dress in goop suits which feature a large head made from a flour sack or a pillow case covering the upper part of the body. A detailed explanation of this costume and the novelty numbers done with it is given on page 150. A pair of long-handled underwear makes a basic clown costume when stuffed and accented by a bright-colored net skirt and neck ruffle. Huge bow ties, tremendously long and wide cravats, loud vests, and baggy trousers and knickers are great laugh getters. Old funny hats can always be used for humorous effects.

The conventional clown costume is a large, loose-fitting suit with a ruffled collar. It can be made from almost any material as long as the colors and patterns are bright and contrasting. Commercial patterns for making such suits can be found in many pattern books

at local dry goods counters. A novel variation of the clown suit is the upside-down clown. This is really a right-side-up child who wears slippers on his hands and large canvas gloves on his feet. Paint features on a balloon for the clown face and top it with a cone-shaped hat made from heavy paper. The costume can be made from polka dot material or vari-colored striped material; or it can be made using an old sheet which has paper polka dots attached with cellophane tape.

Tramp clowns are among the most famous in all circusdom, and the costumes are very easy to make. Fill any old baggy suit or pair of overalls with pillows or balloons. Oversize shoes and clown or tramp masks can be found at Halloween time at the costume counters. (You will do well to buy these props while they are in stock and save them for your circus.) Clown shoes can be made by filling small salt or sugar sacks half full of rags or old nylons and slipping the end over the toe of a shoe. Attach strings to the sack so it can be tied around the arch and ankles to keep it in place. An alternate method is to cut a piece of plastic, leatherette, or heavy cardboard in the shape of a large shoe and fasten it to the foot with elastic webbing or string. Swimming fins can also be used or slip a pair of Dad's old shoes over the child's own shoes fastening them with heavy twine, a rubber band, or a colorful strip of cloth which can be tied over each instep in a huge bow.

No two bona fide circus clowns paint their faces exactly alike. When the clown makes up his face in a certain way, the make-up is supposed to be his own and is never copied by any other clown. However, white-faced clowns are almost standard in any circus. For this type of make-up the clown should wear a skull cap made of jersey or knit nylon that fits tightly over the hair and around the face. A sleeve of an old, white T-shirt makes a good cap. After snipping out oval openings for the ears, gather the armhole end of the sleeve and pull it down snugly over the head. To start the make-up, have your clown grimace or twist his face so that you can find the right lines or expressions from which to build his funny face. Cover his face with clown-white (white grease paint available at costume houses) and blend into over-all smoothness. Wrap a soft cloth or cleansing tissue over your index finger and outline the eyebrows, nose, and mouth. You will want to do some experimenting here. If you don't like the face you've drawn, refill the areas with more clown white and start over. When you've achieved a satisfactory design, fill in the design with bright make-up. Gay red noses and mouths are funny as are big arched eyebrows, but a wide black mouth outlined in red with corners lifted in a huge smile is hilarious. You may want to add one or two large teeth. After the face is completed, set the make-up by generously powdering it with talcum powder. Whisk away the excess powder. Grease paint can easily be removed by using cold cream and cleansing tissues. A number of suggestions for clown faces are illustrated below.

Clown caricatures are always entertaining, with burlesques of women or famous people most popular. Numerous trick items, such as cans of nuts which when opened spout forth yards of cloth-covered spring "snakes," can be used as props for the clowns. Novelty stores offer a wide selection of such items. Be very careful to avoid any embarrassment that might be caused by props that are not in good taste.

Clowns can perform a tumbling act with great dexterity and skill if they have had a little experience in trampoline, tumbling, or pyramid building. Of course they will "ham" it up for all its worth!

A suggested clown stunt follows: Two clowns walk to the front of the audience. One carries a glass of water; the other carries a bucket containing bits of torn-up newspaper. The second clown asks the

first, "What are you doing with all that water? You going fishing?" The first clown says, "I don't have enough water to go fishing, but it looks like you have." The second clown answers, "You don't have the intelligence to catch a fish with a net at a fish hatchery!" The first clown indignantly throws his glass of water right into the face of the other clown who retaliates by picking up his bucket and throwing its contents towards the audience. If it is done convincingly and quickly, the normal audience reaction will be to scream because the torn-up paper momentarily resembles water as it comes flying through the air.

Here is another routine. Two clowns who know the trick hold the ends of a long piece of string at either end of a row. They pretend to carry on a "telephone conversation." All the guests sitting along one row hold the string between their teeth if they wish to hear a most interesting conversation. After a short, humorous conversation between the players holding the string, one asks the other, "Where have you been?" The answer, "Fishing." "Catch anything?" "Yes, a whole string of suckers!"

You can have giant clowns walking on stilts with long clown pants covering the stilts. Other clown suggestions are found on pages 150 and 172 (midget, goop).

Folk Dances and Drills

These can be a colorful part of your circus if you have a group of dancers dressed in native costumes who can do folk dances. Though this is not a standard part of a circus performance, it will provide color and interest if done well. Many communities and schools teach children these dances. Irish dancers, Spanish dancers, Scottish dancers, Oriental dancers, or Hawaiian dancers will all be most interesting. The costumes can be made simply. For example, the Hawaiian skirt can be made from green crêpe paper sewn to a pink band. Colorful crêpe-paper leis and flowers add an authentic touch.

Twirling Units and Drills

Many young people can do baton twirling demonstrations either as individuals or units. If such a group is available in your area, have it give a demonstration for your circus. The gay costumes, flags, and banners are excellent for a circus, and the drills will be most interesting if accompanied by music from the record player. Children love this!

The following acts and novelty numbers which are suitable for the amateur circus need little or no rehearsal:

"And now we present our next feature attraction!"

Sandra the Snake Charmer

"Ladies and Gentlemen, may we have your attention. Notice how this little lady fearlessly and courageously handles these deadly snakes, permitting them to curl around her neck and over her arms. In that basket she has deadly pythons, rattlesnakes, and the most vicious snakes ever to be assembled together by one lady. Now, Sandra, pick up one of the snakes in your basket and show the audience how it wiggles." Sandra holds a wooden segmented snake by the mid-section and wiggles it back and forth to give a realistic snake movement. She continues to handle the snakes by wrapping them around her neck and arms and she even puts the head of one of the snakes into her mouth as the ringmaster announces, "And there you have it, folks. Let's give Sandra a big hand! Thank you, Sandra, for that marvelous performance and display of intrepid courage!"

Costume: Sandra the Snake Charmer can wear any bright-colored skirt and blouse with costume jewelry, or she may be outfitted in an oriental-style costume with midriff top and pantaloons. A gypsy costume with large dangling gold or rhinestone earrings would be suitable. Dark skin make-up and oriental features may be applied if desired. She should carry a wicker basket full of dime-store, brown and green snakes, either rubber and/or segmented wooden ones. Of course, a large variety of snakes will add to the novelty and effectiveness of the act. If you want to make your own snakes, hinge pieces of rubber or plastic tubing (such as garden hoses are made of) together. Telephone companies occasionally have large quantities of plastic tubing which have been discarded after cable connections are made. These can be realistically painted to resemble snakes.

Another snake-charming act features an Indian fakir who demonstrates how music can charm even the most vicious snake. He is dressed in a white or colored breech cloth and a white turban. He has a basket of snakes and a toy flute or symphonette and he sits

down cross-legged on the stage or lawn area in front of the audience. As he raises the flute to his lips and begins to play (an accompaniment may be given behind the scenes), the snake rises up from the basket to the tune of the flute. The trick is that one end of a long, thin, black thread is tied to the end of the flute while the other is attached to the head of the snake so that the movement of the flute determines the movement of the snake. If you can't find wooden snakes, make your own by wrapping green or yellow crêpe paper around a broom handle. Paste the seams and crush down. Remove the broom handle. Put a thin wire through the crushed tube of paper and twist it into a snake-like position. Add paper eyes and fangs for effect.

Bareback Riders

The above act can be followed by a dazzling display of beautiful bareback riders. The clowns, acting as stagehands, can bring out the horses which are sawhorses all rigged up with paper-sack heads and rope manes and tails. If you feel it desirable to give the bareback riders a substantial footing, widen the sawhorse back by nailing a four or six inch board across the top. Three or four little girls beautifully dressed in ballet costumes mount the horses, balance, pirouette, and show off lovely dancing positions while the record player plays suitable music such as "Skaters' Waltz" or "Les Sylphides." If ballet costumes cannot be borrowed or improvised, Sunday best dresses can be worn or costumes may be salvaged from dancing classes. Even leotards and a short full skirt will do very well in this role. The ringmaster announces the act in glowing terms and builds it up with a commentary on how adroit the girls are in balancing so perfectly on the galloping horses!

Acrobats and Tumblers

Many schools teach tumbling and pyramid building in their physical education classes. Perhaps some of the children in your neighborhood are proficient in this. If not, a group of children can plan to do simple tumbling acts and build pyramids with very little practice. Since the trampoline has become so popular, many children can perform various stunts on this also. Costumes can be simple play suits or regular gym suits. You may want your clowns to take part in this act and ham it up with simple rolls or dives, somersaults, cartwheels, and barrel and spider walks.

Siamese Twins

"Next, Ladies and Gentlemen, we present from far off Bangkok the famous Royal Siamese Twins!" The twins are two boys of approximately the same size and coloring who are dressed in a single large-size T-shirt. (Ask a men's clothing department for the largest size it has in stock.) Both boys have their heads projecting from the neck of the shirt, and the twin on the left has his left arm in the left sleeve while the right twin has his right arm projecting from the right sleeve of the shirt.

The ringmaster has the boys demonstrate various ways in which they co-ordinate their actions. For example, he'll say something like this: "Now, boys, I want you to show us what you would do if the one on the left wants to scratch his left ear with his right arm. Suppose you show us how it's done!" There will undoubtedly be some confusion as each tries to decide which one will use which hand to scratch which ear! The ringmaster continues to talk the boys through several other maneuvers such as tying their shoes with each boy using one hand. As a finale the ringmaster could have them play a short number on an instrument such as a concertina, a violin, bongo drums, a guitar, or any other instrument that requires two hands to play!

This laugh-provoking act is followed by a demonstration of the wild animals which is really the heart of a circus.

Wild Animal Act

"And now, Ladies and Gentlemen, may we have your undivided attention. We are about to present the greatest array of ferocious and vicious wild animals in captivity! Bring on the wild animals and their famous trainer!"

The wild animals and the tamer come into the center of the arena. If desired, the ringmaster wearing his breeches, boots, white shirt, and bright vest or flowing cape may double as the tamer with just the addition of a toy cap pistol in a holster and a whip in one hand and a hoop in the other. The clowns or stage hands bring on the rest of his "props"—a small child's chair to be used in keeping the animals under control, and a small round tub (either a small laundry tub or a wooden tub painted in bright circus colors of red, yellow, and blue) which the animals use in performing their tricks.

The various wild animals such as lions, panthers, tigers, and leopards can easily be costumed in simple one-piece suits, patterns for which can be found in the pattern books. Or pajamas can easily be turned into animal costumes by adding a few distinguishing features such as spots, stripes, or manes. For example, dye the pajamas yellow and add a cotton mop mane for a lion. For a panther, dye the pajamas black and add a helmet-type hood or a mask. Many stores carry regular children's pajamas which resemble animal skins, and these make ideal costumes. See page 129 for paper animal costumes.

When the animals and tamer are in the arena, the announcer can explain in excited tones just what dare-devil stunts are being performed as the animals go through a series of tricks and stunts that are found in the repertoire of a genuine lion tamer. The tamer cracks his long whip, shoots his gun, and fends off the ferocious beasts with a small chair. The animals growl at each other and snap and lunge at the tamer. With a little practice, even the tamest amateur lion can develop a fine snarl! The tamer now has the animals jump through hoops, stand on small tubs, roll over, catch balls, and hold the tail of the preceding animal in their mouths and go around in a ring. The tamer can even show his fearlessness by putting his hand into the mouths of the ferocious beasts! For a flourishing finish, the animals play leap frog with the tamer eventually joining the group.

Be sure to intersperse these acts with a few clown antics. This would be a good time to have your tramp clown go around and sorrowfully try to find a friend in the audience. If possible, he should look pathetic and sad at the same time that he uses some little trick or stunt to catch the audience off guard, for this will bring a hearty laugh from everyone. Some short stunts such as the following may be used:

Put the tips of all your fingers, including thumbs, together. Now, tell another person that you are going to crack an egg on his head. Make one sharp downward motion until it touches his head lightly, then slowly expand the fingers, and let them lightly touch the hair as they expand. This is to simulate the feeling of having the raw egg running down the hair. The effect is amazing!

"I have here in my pocket something that you never saw before and will never see again. In fàct, nobody (even I) has ever seen it before, and nobody will ever see it again!"

(You take out a peanut in the shell, crack the shell, show the group the peanut, then eat it. They never saw it before—will never see it again.)

Herman Hercules

Next the ringmaster announces the appearance of Herman Hercules, the strong man. Such amazing feats of strength he performs! Not since the days of Samson has anyone seen an exhibit to equal this!

Herman's costume consists of a long pair of drawers and a sweat

shirt stuffed with rags to make huge, bulging muscles in all the right places. Over his drawers he can wear a bright-colored pair of trunks or boxing shorts.

He struts around and poses, flexing his muscles and showing off his magnificent build. The announcer says, "And now six of our strongest stage hands will carry in Herman's props." The clowns, feigning great effort and with much huffing and puffing, carry in a bar-bell which is actually a broom stick with round oatmeal boxes fastened to each end to resemble weights. These are marked "500 lbs." The announcer continues: "Now, Herman, do you think you can lift this tremendous weight all alone?" Herman nods in agreement. Then pretending great effort, he ultimately succeeds in lifting the bar-bell high over his head. Then as the audience applauds wildly, he slowly and carefully puts it down. This is followed by Herman lifting the 1000 lb. weights with one little finger. These weights are made from black cardboard as illustrated. They are brought onto the stage in a wagon and tugged across the arena by a crew of stagehands. Again the audience shows appreciation by generous applause.

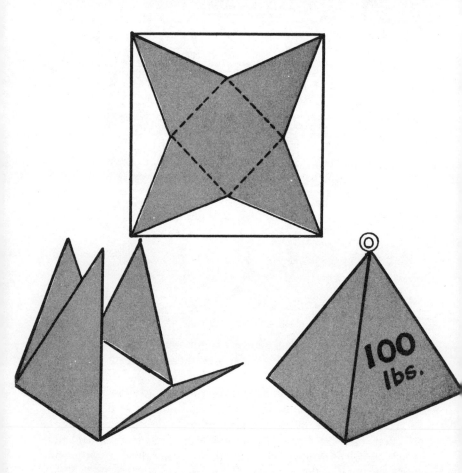

The announcer says, "Now, folks, Herman is going to perform a feat unparalleled in circus history. With his own bare hands he will attempt to bend a piece of steel pipe!" At this point Herman passes a length of pipe approximately 12" long and 1" in diameter among the spectators. After the audience has examined the pipe, he takes it and strikes it against some hard object and returns to his place in the center of the ring. Turning his back to the audience, he quickly substitutes a piece of rubber hose for the steel pipe. He does this by slipping the steel pipe up one sleeve while quickly removing the rubber pipe from the other sleeve. This is done as unobtrusively as possible. The rubber hose is the same length as the steel pipe. It has been painted with aluminum paint to make it look like metal and has been stuffed with pliable wire so that when it bends, it will retain its shape and not snap back. "Now, Ladies and Gentlemen," continues the announcer, "Watch Herman bend that tremendous piece of pipe. Watch him carefully! Is he going to do it? Wow! Just look at that! He did it! A great big hand for Herman Hercules, the strongest man in the world!"

As Herman retires from the ring, a clown comes in and lightly picks up the weights and barbells and trips casually off the stage to the amusement of the entire crowd.

Bearded Lady

Herman is followed by the freak Bearded Lady. "Introducing one of the amazing features of the ages, we proudly present Whiska Stubble, the Bearded Lady!" A girl dressed in any old-style clothing comes into the ring wearing a wig and a luxurious beard made of a light-weight string mop died yellow, brown, or black, whichever color matches her hair. (You may want to rent a beard and a wig from a costume house or beards and wigs in various styles can sometimes be purchased at a novelty store.)

"Believe it or not, Ladies and Gentlemen, this little lady started shaving at the age of three but stopped at sixteen when a Gillette salesman got lost in her beard. Take a bow, Whiska."

Growing Machine

The ringmaster next announces: "Friends, you will now see one of the most astounding developments of modern science. The stage-hands will now help Professor Feffenfloofer bring in his amazing invention, the Growing Machine!" The clowns pull onto the stage a wagon on which there is a large, corrugated box labeled "Growing

Machine." The professor (or the announcer) explains that nuclear power has now been developed to make things grow. To demonstrate, he drops a tennis ball into the machine. Inside the box a small boy is hidden who throws out a volleyball! The professor drops in a piece of string—out comes a length of rope. Into the machine the professor next puts a small book and out pops a large book. Finally the professor tosses in a baby doll. Out jumps the boy (dressed in baby clothes and bonnet like the doll) who throws his arms around the professor and calls, "Daddy!"

Midget Clown

The next interlude features a midget clown act. It requires a curtain backdrop which can be made from an old sheet. A boy dressed as a clown kneels in front of the sheet which has holes cut out for his feet to extend through. He has large, clown shoes tied on to his knees. The midget can tell a joke or a story or sing a funny song. A clown trick such as the following can be used:

This is a tricky trick. It may actually take people a little while to get onto it. Tell them that you can prove that you have eleven fingers.

"You say I have ten?" you say. "All right, we'll see."

Then you start counting, beginning with the thumb.

"You say ten, so I'll start there and go backwards." Then you count, "Ten, nine, eight, seven, six" which of course is the count for the fingers of one hand. Then say, "All right, there were six, and I have five fingers on this hand, so that makes a total of eleven!"

They may want to go through it again. Finally someone discovers that you have tricked them a little.

Junius the Juggler

"And now we present to you Junius the Juggler—the greatest juggler of our time!" Junius enters wearing dark trousers, white shirt, and bright red cummerbund. A bolero jacket and colorful braid would add to the costume but is not necessary. Junius balances the cups and plates as shown in the illustration below on his finger and with moderate practice, he can balance them on his chin. He performs all the skillful maneuvers of a juggler keeping his paraphernalia balanced. The paper plates and cups used in the act are fastened both

to each other and to the tray by a string which runs down the handle. The string is secured by an elastic band at the base of the handle or is attached to a ring which Junius can hold firmly with his finger. At the end of the act, after thunderous applause, Junius hands the prop to a stagehand, releasing the string. The stagehand puts the prop over his shoulder and carries it off stage with the cups and plates dangling down his back.

Junius then does his famous plate-spinning trick. He is handed two decorated dowel sticks to which paper plates, face down, have been thumbtacked slightly off center. The plates will spin when the dowel is turned and they should be decorated with bright-colored spots to add to the illusion.

Lulu the Fat Lady

"For a Big Thrill, Friends, we present a Big Girl, Lulu the Fat Lady. Come out Lulu and take a bow!" Lulu enters the ring wearing a huge dress preferably loud in color and design. She has been either padded with pillows, front and back, which are secured by a string around her waist and fastened at the shoulders with pins, or her dress is stuffed with balloons. "Lulu just had a snack. Do you know what she ate? Fourteen hot dogs, six quarts of lemonade, and two and a half gallons of ice cream—just for an afternoon snack—her third since lunch! She's going on a diet tomorrow; she's cutting down her eggs from twelve to nine—dozen that is."

If Lulu is stuffed with balloons, you could have the clowns pop some as she leaves the stage. It's a quick way to help her reduce!

Educated Horse

"Eddie the Educated Horse is our next feature attraction, Ladies and Gentlemen! We have gone to great expense to bring him to you." Eddie, the horse, is dressed in an athletic warm-up suit or long underwear which can be dyed brown or black if desired. If the suit is left white, pinto patches should be sewed on it. The head pattern is illustrated on page 153. Or an ordinary paper bag large enough to fit over a person's head can be decorated with eyes, ears, nostrils, and mouth and used for a mask.

The ringmaster directs Eddie the Horse in demonstrations of his

intellect. A number of colored scarves (red, white, green, blue, and yellow) are used by Eddie in answering questions such as: "What are the colors of the American Flag? What color is the grass?" Additional props are a large cardboard clock used for telling time and some cardboard squares with large numbers painted on them which are used in answering questions about addition and subtraction. The ringmaster asks Eddie "How many is 2 plus 3?" Eddie answers by stomping his feet the correct number of times or pointing to the appropriate square. At the conclusion of the routine, Eddie bows to the audience and acknowledges the applause and exits from the ring.

An educated dog could perform the same type of stunts in addition to answering questions such as: "What's on a house?" "Ruff, Ruff, Ruff!" "What grows on a tree?" "Bark, Bark, Bark!"

High-Stepping Horses

Any number of performers can join in this act. Horses can be made with broom-handle bodies, paper-sack heads, rope manes, and shoelace bridles, or horse bodies and heads can be cut from large sheets of heavy cardboard. Paint features on the cardboard head and make the body double so that the rider stands inside holding the horse at waist height by means of rope handles or suspender straps. The riders prance around the ring to brisk lively music such as "1812 Overture" or "William Tell Overture." The riders should go around the ring in single file prancing with spirit and zest and then doing a few paces in slow motion. As a finale, they might swing out into various formations and drills exhibiting remarkable precision and horsemanship. Even though the announcer can cue them in at the right time, it would be well to have the riders rehearse their maneuvers in advance so that they will do them well at the performance.

Trained Seals

"Now the trained seals perform for your entertainment. They are trained to do various balancing feats that require great coordination! Here they come into the ring! Give them a big hand, folks." Very young children from three to six years of age can easily do the simple tricks necessary for this act. Each child wears a colored crêpe-paper ruffle around his neck. These are made by stitching down the center of a length of crêpe paper and then gathering the ruffle to the desired fullness. Fasten strings or tape to the ends and use them as ties. Hats for the seals are made from cottage cheese cartons painted in bright colors. These are fastened under the chin by stapling an elastic band on each side of the carton and then tying a heavy string to the elastics. This allows for give-and-take yet the hat stays on snuggly. Each seal holds a round inflated balloon by his teeth. To the accompaniment of background music, the trainer talks the seals through their act. In uniform precision, they "balance" the balloons on their noses, roll over, keel over, and flap their flippers. They also catch paper or plastic fish thrown to them by the trainer.

Minstrel Show

The announcer introduces the next number as an old-fashioned minstrel act. This can be a real minstrel show that has been rehearsed and prepared beforehand from one of the many scripts available for this type of performance. A series of jokes which are funny and in good taste should be given by the End Men and the Interlocutor, followed by a musical number or two. The musical numbers can feature a chorus or individual performances on the banjo, harmonica, or guitar. If you don't want to put on a regular minstrel show, a good minstrel quartet would be sufficient. The performers can wear dark suits. Large bright-colored bow ties of paper or cloth and white canvas gloves accent the costumes. Traditional black make-up may be used or minstrel masks can be made very inexpensively from paper sacks as illustrated. Paste black paper ears, blue crêpe-paper ties, and yellow paper top hats on the sack. Cut holes for the eyes and mouth and paint the features' bright red and white. A simple minstrel act suitable for children is printed below.

THE MINSTREL SHOW

"All right, Ladies and Gentlemen, will you give us your attention, please? Here you have the greatest sideshow attraction ever presented on the American midway. In just a moment we're going to have a great, free show for you right here in front. Here they are now. Give them a big hand! You see before you, friends, the Sunny Southland Minstrels, the greatest aggregation of black-face stars ever assembled. They have just arrived from Hollywood. You'll laugh, you'll cry, you'll thrill to those inimitable melodies of the Southland sung as you've never heard them sung before! Strike up a chord!"

Modern Minstrels

Characters: Mr. Boodle—Interlocutor
Mr. Bones & Mr. Moans—End Men
Girls' Chorus—Any number
Boys' Chorus—Any number
Special Performers—Any number

Setting: Arrange bleachers or chairs on stage for the choruses. Mr. Boodle has a chair at stage center. Mr. Bones and Mr. Moans are at the extreme right and left of stage. Your artists can devise a spectacular backdrop if time and interest permit.

Costumes: Costumes offer plenty of chance for originality. The group that puts on the show should get together and decide how much costuming they can manage. The boys could wear white trousers, white shirts, purple bow ties, white gloves, and top hats made from tagboard and black or purple construction paper. The three main characters could be costumed like the other boys with the addition of purple vests and canes. The girls might wear white full skirts, purple blouses with long full sleeves, white ties, white gloves, and tall top hats. Or, you can plan special costumes for the three main characters only.

(Entire group is seated on the stage with Mr. Boodle in the center and Mr. Bones and Mr. Moans on either end. A musical selection is being played as the curtain opens. All clap hands in time to the music and sing one verse.)

Mr. Boodle: (*rising as he makes this rhymed announcement*)

Well, what d'ye know? What d'ye know?
Look who's come to see our show!
Place full of people, for goodness' sake!
If we'd have known you were commin', we'd have baked a cake!
Now, sit right there till the show is through
And clap your hands—if you like what we do!
Mr. Bones!

Mr. Bones: (rises) Yes, sir, Mr. Boodle!

Mr. Boodle: How are you this afternoon, Mr. Bones?

Mr. Bones: Well, to tell the truth, I'm still wondering!

Mr. Boodle: Oh! Wondering? What are you wondering about?

Mr. Bones: Well, I'm wondering what you were looking for when I saw you downtown today.

Mr. Boodle: Oh, I was hunting the First National Bank.

Mr. Bones: Did you find it?

Mr. Boodle: No, I didn't. Can you direct me to it?

Mr. Bones: I can for a quarter.

Mr. Boodle: A quarter? Isn't that pretty high?

Mr. Bones: Not for a Bank Director. (*Sits.*)

(*Wait for laughs after each joke.*)

Mr. Boodle: Well, Mr. Moans, how are you this afternoon?

Mr. Moans: (*rises*) I feel just like a pair of tonsils.

Mr. Boodle: A pair of tonsils? Now, how's that?

Mr. Moans: (*with facial expression*) Sorter down in the mouth. (*Sits.*)

(*Wait for laughs.*)

Mr. Boodle: Well, Mr. Moans, we'll have to see what we can do to cure you. How about listening to (pupil's name) play (names musical selection)?

(*Pupil plays.*)

Mr. Bones: You know, Mr. Boodle, I'm very, very tired this afternoon.

Mr. Boodle: Why are you so tired, Mr. Bones?

Mr. Bones: I've been looking for a job all day.

Mr. Boodle: Indeed! What kind of job do you hope to find?

Mr. Bones: I want a job in the post office.

Mr. Boodle: To hold a job in the post office, you must be a very responsible person.

Mr. Bones: Oh, I'm very responsible all right. Why, every place I ever worked something went wrong—and they always said I was responsible.

Mr. Boodle: Ladies and gentlemen! We now present to you our blue-eyed pianist (pupil's name) who will play for you (names selection).

(*Pupil plays.*)

Mr. Moans: It's just beautiful. I tell you it's just beautiful!

Mr. Boodle: Yes, that number was beautiful, Mr. Moans.

Mr. Moans: Oh, that too. But the way it flies is really beautiful.

Mr. Boodle: What do you mean? What's beautiful?

Mr. Moans: My new airplane. Every afternoon, I fly over the town in it.

Mr. Boodle: Dear me, that must be delightful!

Mr. Moans: Oh, do you want to fly (do you wanna fly)?

Mr. Boodle: Yes, indeed.

Mr. Moans: Okay, I'll catch one for you. (*Gestures.*)

Mr. Boodle: That's ridiculous! And what's more I think you don't know anything about flying. Ladies and gentlemen! At this time we present for your enjoyment (*gives pupil's name and nature of the act*).

Mr. Bones: Mr. Boodle, did you know that Mr. Watson who runs the pet store can put a tail on a dog?

Mr. Boodle: I never heard of such a thing! What makes you think he could put a tail on a dog?

Mr. Bones: Well, I can't figure it out but when I was in his store the other day I heard him say that he had a license to retail dogs!

(*Mr. Boodle announces next program number.*)

Mr. Boodle: Yes, that was very fine, very fine indeed. Yes, yes, indeed! Most extraordinary!

Mr. Moans: How come you use such big words?

Mr. Boodle: Everybody should learn to use big words as well as little ones. It's important to have a good vocabulary.

Mr. Moans: Oh, I know all about words.

Mr. Boodle: You know all about words, Mr. Moans?

Mr. Moans: Yep, I know all about words.

Mr. Boodle: Well, we'll see about that. Here's a test for you. Use the word "climate" in a sentence.

Mr. Moans: That's too easy! There's a tree in my backyard, but I can't climb it.

Mr. Boodle: That's terrible. You must know more than that.

Mr. Moans: I think so too. Try me on something else.

Mr. Boodle: Well, give me a sentence using the word "design."

Mr. Moans: Lemme see, lemme see! Oh, I know! (*Jubilantly.*) Never cross the street without de sign! (*Laughs, as others applaud.*)

(*Mr. Boodle announces the next number.*)

Mr. Boodle: It's wonderful to have talent, isn't it? I often wish I had talent, don't you, Mr. Bones?

Mr. Bones: Oh, I'm very talented myself.

Mr. Boodle: What can you do?

Mr. Bones: Me? Why I can carry fourteen cups and seven plates in my right hand.

Mr. Boodle: And what do you do with your left hand?

Mr. Bones: I use that to pick up the pieces!

(*Mr. Boodle hastily announces the next entertainment feature.*)

Mr. Boodle: Mr. Moans, what is that book you are so interested in? Not a joke book, I hope?

Mr. Moans: No, Mr. Boodle, it isn't. I read a book every day.

Mr. Boodle: You read a book every day? What about?

Mr. Moans: Oh, science, geography—natural history—

Mr. Boodle: So you know something about natural history?

Mr. Moans: Oh, I know all about natural history.

Mr. Boodle: Well, can you answer this: Do we get fur from a tiger?

Mr. Moans: We sure do! We get as fur from a tiger as possible. (*Laughs loudly as he claps dramatically.*)

(*Mr. Boodle announces next number.*)

Mr. Bones: Mr. Boodle, did you hear about all the excitement at our house last night?

Mr. Boodle: Excitement at your house, Mr. Bones? Now what could excite such a sleepyhead as you? (*Scratches head and thinks.*) Is your brother in the hospital?

Mr. Bones: No, sir, he isn't. But my sister came home last night. She's been in the hospital three years.

Mr. Boodle: Your sister has been in the hospital three years? What's been the matter with her?

Mr. Bones: Nothing! She's been studying to be a nurse.

(*Mr. Boodle announces next number.*)

Mr. Boodle: (*as entire company stands*)
Well, what d'ye know? What d'ye know?
Now we've come to the end of our show!
Thanks for coming! Thanks from me
And thanks from the entire company!

(*All sing a favorite group or community song.*)

Other minstrel acts are available at libraries and drama distributing companies. Some good minstrels for children are:

Jolly Juvenile Minstrels by Grace Gaffney.
Juvenile Blackface Minstrels.
Newsboys' and Bootblacks' Minstrel Show.

Amayzo the Clown

"And now Amayzo the Clown with his Magic Balloons. Amayzo is holding a large red balloon in his hand and he is going to change its color to yellow right before your very eyes. This transformation takes place with a loud noise. Watch carefully, folks, you don't want to miss one second of this incredible stunt!"

Amayzo's balloon is actually three balloons in one. Three balloons are inserted inside each other and then inflated. To do this, insert a pencil (eraser first) into a light-colored balloon and force it inside a medium-shaped balloon. Repeat this, inserting the second balloon inside a third balloon which is larger and of a darker color so that the inner balloons will not show through. Inflate the outer balloon first folding the ends of the inner balloons back over the stem of the outer balloon. Repeat the process inflating each balloon in succession. Make the outer balloon an inch or two larger than the intermediate one and the intermediate a little larger than the inside one so that when Amayzo uses a pin to pop each balloon in turn, only the outer balloon will burst.

Tattooed Man

"One of the most unusual—even fantastic—characters in our circus troupe is the Tattooed Man. He has been all over the world, and brought forth exclamations from everyone who has viewed this extraordinary person."

The Tattooed Man makes his appearance wearing a bathrobe or dressing gown which he removes revealing swim trunks or shorts and a body covered with tattoos of every description. Snakes, flowers, ships, flags, and all kinds of designs can be painted on with poster or show card paints. (These can be easily washed off later.) If a ship with waves under it is painted on the Tattooed Man's chest, he can delight his audience by flexing his abdominal muscles so that the waves will move and the ship will "sail."

Tightrope Walker

"And now, Ladies and Gentlemen, you will see one of our most spectacular attractions. You have no doubt noticed the tightrope stretched high across the performers' area, and you probably have not dared to believe that some of our beautiful stars would attempt to walk that rope. Now, Ladies and Gentlemen, it is my pleasure to introduce to you these attractive darlings of the tight-wire, Balancina and Kerplop. Come and take a bow, girls. Clowns, will you please bring the ladder so that these daring performers can ascend to their position on the rope? Now, clowns, please place it so that they can step from the top of the ladder right directly onto the rope. All right! Balancina, are you going to be first? Ladies and gentlemen, we would like to have perfect quiet so that there will be no disturbance at all for a feat which requires steady nerves, great courage, and skill. Now, Ladies and Gentlemen, you will observe that Balancina is at the top of the ladder and touching the rope with her foot while her sister, Kerplop, is ascending the ladder ready to follow Balancina. There appears to be a little skepticism on the part of certain members of the audience as to whether these girls can really walk across on that tightrope. Let's see by a show of hands how many of you think they *cannot* do it? Oh, so many of you doubt their ability. All right, stage hands, make sure that the rope is fixed so they can perform this outstanding feat of daring and skill."

(At this point the stage hands release the rope at one end which allows the rope to fall in a straight line on the grass or floor. The girls descend the ladder and begin walking across the rope still pretending that it is a feat requiring great balancing skill. They may carry small umbrellas or long poles to help them keep their balance.)

"Let's give these ladies a real round of applause, Ladies and Gentlemen, and a particular round of applause by those who were skeptical about this performance. Thank you, girls. Thank you very much!"

Another way to stage this act is to stretch a long strip of innertube rubber between two chairs. When the performer steps on the tubing, her weight stretches it to the floor. The performers should balance precariously and almost overbalance, catch themselves with great relief, and go through all the maneuvers of a bona fide highwire act!

The tightrope walkers may wear ballet costumes or pretty pastel dresses. Flowers and ribbons in their hair plus make-up and costume jewelry will help them feel that they are really big-time circus stars!

Hair-Cutting Machine

This little novelty act is similar to the growing-machine stunt. Clowns come on stage pulling a wagon which has a large box on it; the box is painted and labeled "Hair-Cutting Machine." The announcer says, "The clowns are now bringing in their astounding, mechanical device that will automatically cut hair. Notice the large head of hair that Shaggy Haggy has. It closely resembles a kitchen mop! Don't be fearful, Shaggy. Put your head in the opening." The sound of machinery (such as an egg beater whirring) is heard. When Shaggy removes his head, the wig is gone and his head is covered with a tight-fitting, skin-colored cap (such as a bathing cap) which gives the appearance of a bald head. Shaggy takes one look at himself in the mirror and runs off stage screaming!

Magician Act

"And now, Ladies and Gentlemen, we present Can-do the Magician. While he is setting up his table to show you his famous tricks which prove that the hand is quicker than the eye, it is my pleasure to report to you that Can-do's wife is a magician also. On their way

down here today, she turned her car into a telephone pole! And now Can-do is ready and will perform his amazing act."

At this point the boy or girl scheduled to do this act performs whatever tricks or stunts he has selected. With a little practice, most young people can do very well with the tricks that are available in magic or trick shops. Some of these items include handkerchiefs that change colors by being drawn inside themselves through a ring, disappearing sponges hidden inside a cup, a pitcher of water which continues to have water in it even though it appears drained each time it is inverted, and artificial flowers which appear magically from inside the magician's coat or vest.

The magician could wear a large dark coat folded at the front to look like a cutaway and a large derby or top hat. His assistant can be dressed in a gypsy or oriental costume. A microphone would be an asset for this particular act as the audience should clearly hear the magician explain his magical feats.

Clairvoyant

Part of the magician act can include fortune telling and mind reading. The announcer explains: "For the next act we will need your cooperation. Our mind reader needs some minds to read so we hope you have brought yours with you." Simple mind-reading stunts can easily be done by Can-do and his assistant. One such stunt follows:

The assistant gives blank strips of paper to eight different people in the audience. Each is instructed to write a question and the correct answer on his paper, sign his name, and then fold his paper so that the assistant can't read the name. The assistant collects the slips in a basket or hat and gives them one at a time to the magician who places the folded slip to his forehead, closes his eyes, concentrates and then amazes the audience by stating what is written on the paper. Actually the first question-answer is pre-arranged with some member of the audience so that slip number one is palmed and slip number two is substituted. Hence, when Can-do puts the first slip to his head, it is actually slip number two. After mind-reading the first slip of paper, he opens it and reads it to check if the answer is correct. In reality he is reading the question and answer on slip number two. Therefore, when he goes through the motions of mind-reading question number two, he has slip number three at his forehead. After stating question and answer number two, he checks by opening the slip and reading number three. He repeats this performance with each slip of paper always reading beforehand the question and answer to be used next. If done well, this can completely baffle the audience.

Another trick is to ask who in the audience would like to have his palm "read." Those who raise their hands are approached, and the assistant paints their palms with a dab of red poster paint or lipstick! This little stunt would be good for a clown to do after boasting that he can tell fortunes!

Cutting-In-Two Act

The announcer says in a somber voice, "Now, Ladies and Gentlemen, if there are those in the audience who are sensitive or squeamish, we suggest you leave before the next act takes place. We are now going to present to you that most daring, most spectacular of all

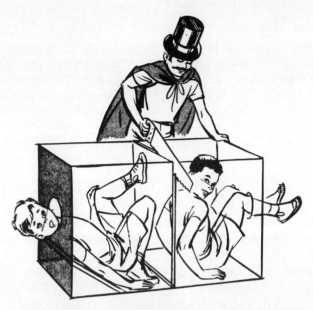

acts—the *sawing-in-two* of a boy! Ladies and Gentlemen, right here before you, in front of your very eyes you will see this astounding performance. Don't go away!" At this point, the stage hands wheel in a wagon which has a large box on a platform. A boy's head protrudes from one end of the box and a boy's feet from the other. The magician who is to do the sawing flexes the saw, tests it for sharpness, and flourishes it in front of the audience. The boy in the box smiles at the audience, moves his feet, and shows that he is very much alive! The magician then proceeds to saw through the box with great dexterity while the boy winces occasionally. The secret of this most sensational of all stage illusions lies in the setup used. Two boxes are joined together with masking tape and painted to look like one long box. Each box contains a boy, and the head and hands of one boy protrude from one box while the feet of the other boy dangle from the other box as illustrated. The saw, of course, comes down between the two boys. After the sawing is completed, the wagon is wheeled away by the stage hands. It provides a good laugh if one of the boxes bumps off the wagon and a boy jumps out and hustles off the stage!

Invisible Man

Another clever, laugh-provoking stunt is the "Invisible Man." Can-do explains in glowing terms that he is now going to give one of the most uncanny demonstrations ever seen. To accomplish this feat, he has the stage hands bring in a chair and place it in the center of the stage. The stage hands then bring out a large sheet and hold it in front of the chair so that no one can see the chair. Can-do then makes mysterious sounds and gestures with his hands. Suddenly the sheet is whisked away, and there is the "Invisible Man." You can't see him, but he's there!

Wild Man from Borneo

"And now, Ladies and Gentlemen, you will see Mobeeko, the Wild Man from Borneo! Mobeeko was captured in the jungles of Borneo and has never been seen in a civilized country before. Don't be alarmed if he appears frightening. He is!" Mobeeko the Wild

Man is costumed in a black suit of longies with furs tacked around his waist. He wears a wig made from a cotton mop dyed black. Huge gold errings dangle from his ears and he has white paint marks on his face. He carries a huge knobby club and makes no sound other than frequent grunts and occasional ear-splitting shrieks as he walks menacingly around.

Mobeeko may do a wild native dance, gnaw on a large bone, or talk in foreign gibberish with many gestures. As he leaves the stage, he is told to say goodby in his native tongue. Waving happily, he says, "Goodby!"

Trained Monkey Act

This performance is given by a child dressed in a monkey suit which can be made by dying a suit of longies brown and tacking brown yarn at the neck, ankles, and wrists. Attach a long stuffed

tail which is supported by a length of wire bent in a curled shape. Brown canvas work gloves are worn on the hands and feet, and a brown skull cap with round brown ears attached complete the costume. The monkey is accompanied by his trainer who wears blue trousers, a red coat, and a cap which can be made from a cottage cheese carton or a round oatmeal box. Paint the cap red and glue a white band labeled "TRAINER" across it.

The trainer leads the monkey in performing various stunts such as riding a small child's tricycle, turning somersaults, and beating a drum. As a reward the monkey gets a banana to eat.

Tallest Midget in the World

"Ladies and Gentlemen, you have heard circuses boast that they have the smallest midget in the world! Well, Ladies and Gentlemen, we have a midget here who will truly amaze you. How tall is our midget? I'll let you guess! Three feet? Two and a half feet? Guess again! All right, I'll tell *you*. We have here not just an ordinary midget, not just about the smallest midget in the world. No, sir. We have here the *tallest* midget in the world! Come out and greet the folks!" At this point an ordinary boy walks out into the ring! This stunt can be reversed and billed as the *Smallest Giant in the World!*

Sharp-Shooting Act

"We now present Wild Bill Boone in a demonstration of the most accurate shooting ever to be seen by man. The stage hands will now carry in the props for Wild Bill." Clowns carry in a cardboard box in which Wild Bill's assistant is concealed. They place several tin cans which have strings attached to them on top of the box. When the stage is set, Wild Bill dressed in a cowboy outfit, comes on flourishing six-shooters and cap guns; he carries a mirror for the trick shooting.

"Now Wild Bill will announce which target he will shoot first." (Bill specifies the first can on the left.) "Ready, aim, fire! Sure enough, there goes the first can!" (The assistant hidden in the box pulls the cans down as Wild Bill shoots, being careful to time his yank with the sound of the shot.) "Which one's next, Bill? The one on the right? Good. Let's fire away! Good for you, Bill, away went that one! Now, how about shooting the others down in rapid succession. Fire away! Bang! Bang! Bang! There they go, folks! What an amazing shooting exhibition! Now Wild Bill is going to set the cans up again and demonstrate his ability to knock them down in quick order with his back to the target; he will hold the gun over his shoulder and look only at the cans through a mirror! Ready now. No distraction from the audience! Everybody quiet? Here we go. Fire away! Let's give him a big hand, folks, for that remarkable display of marksmanship and steady nerves."

"And now, Wild Bill will demonstrate shooting balloons if the stage hands will bring the balloon board." (The balloon board, as illustrated, has a hole behind each balloon so that the assistant can puncture the balloons as the shots are called. It will provide some amusement if the timing is faulty, thereby causing the balloon to pop seconds before or after the shot is fired!) "Okay, Bill, let's see you hit the upper left balloon by looking through the mirror and shooting over your shoulder. Fire away. How's that, folks? Isn't it remarkable? Now the upper right balloon. Now, lower left and lower right." (Bill shoots the balloons specified and ends up by shooting the rest in rapid succession.) "Thank you, thank you, Bill! And now let's have a big hand for Wild Bill Boone, trick shooting artist."

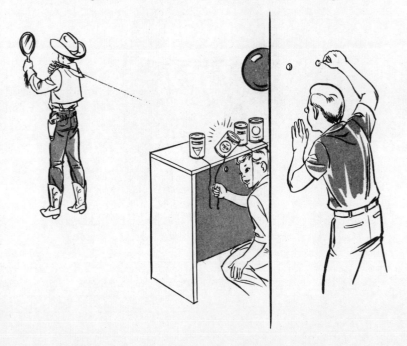

Goop Whistling Act

This number is sure to be a prize winner in any show. The announcer gives a big build up to Whistler's Father. As shown in the illustration, the performer wears a huge hat which covers his head, arms and shoulders, a short jacket with stuffed gloves coming out of the sleeves, a wide shirt collar, a bow tie, and regular trousers and shoes. Paint features as illustrated on his bare skin with grease paint. Be sure the mouth is painted around the navel. A plastic nose and plastic ears, obtainable from a novelty shop or costume house, are fastened on with masking tape in the right places. The performer's arms are raised and crossed over under the big hat as illustrated. To the accompaniment of a whistling record (these are available in record shops) the actor proceeds to pantomime the whistled song by drawing in his stomach muscles and bulging them out. With a little practice this can be done with great "expression" in perfect timing with the recorded music. This novelty act brings the house down!

India Rubber Man

This fantastic character is made by fastening a head made of sturdy paper plates to the end of a broom stick. Cover the broom stick with a length of knit or cotton fabric or use several layers of crushed crêpe paper. Fasten the fabric or paper to the head. Slip the broom stick down through an old lamp shade. Then holding the edge of the lamp shade and the broom stick, have someone drape a coat over the lamp shade and button it securely at the neck. When the broom stick is slowly pushed up, the neck str-et-ch-es up. When the broom stick is brought down, the neck folds up like an accordion.

Trick Animals

If any of the circus performers have animals trained to do stunts and tricks, be sure and include a number in your circus act. Some dogs can do simple tricks like playing dead, jumping through hoops, rolling over, sitting up and begging, and so forth. Give the dog and his master a good snappy introduction.

Freaks

No circus is complete without many freaks and here's another one that will catch the attention of the audience. The actor wears a large clown suit which comes up over his head so that the collar is on top of his head. In his hand he carries a stuffed head which has clown features painted on it. This head may be made using a balloon, a large ball such as a tether ball, or a stuffed paper bag. Put a clown mask on the head and top with a clown cap.

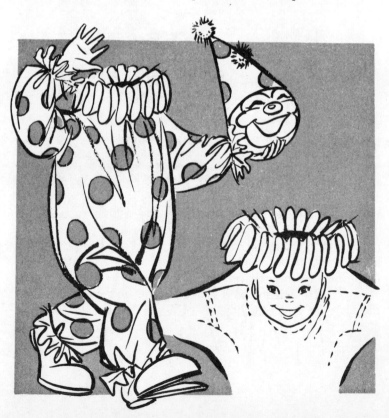

Another circus freak is the half-man-half-woman character who is dressed in one trouser leg and half a skirt. One side of the head has a beard and short hair while the other side is smooth shaven and has long hair. The performer can sing some clever song such as "Side By Side!"

The grand finale for most circuses is usually a rip-roaring, hootin'-shootin' cowboy and Indian battle. Both of these kinds of costumes are very easily made. In fact, many boys will have one or the other on hand. If desired, the Indians can have faces and bodies painted by using grease paint in vivid colors. A band, around the head, holding a single feather or many feathers will do for a headdress. The cowboys usually carry guns while the Indians shoot arrows from their bows. The Indians may perform a war dance before they attack the cowboys. After a swift but fierce battle the Indians are chased off the scene amid much gun smoke from the cowboys. You may want to elaborate on this by depicting a stagecoach hold-up. The Indians threaten to burn the passengers at the stake, but in true Western style they are routed just in time by a band of soldiers or frontiersmen.

Puppet Show

Puppet shows delight audiences of all ages. You may want to include one in your performance. Suggestions for making puppets are found in Chapter Ten.

Ventriloquist

It's hard to say which act will make the biggest hit in your back yard circus, but Mouth-O the Magnificent and his remarkable dummy will be among the funniest. Mouth-O needs no special costume other than a neatly-pressed suit and a great big smile. The dummy works like this: A boy kneeling behind a curtain or sheet puts his head through a convenient slit to provide the dummy with not only a head but a voice. The foundation for the dummy's body (approximately twenty inches tall) is made from wrapping paper. "Dress" the foundation with gummed crêpe and staple the body to the sheet just under the boy's chin. When the ventriloquist sets the dummy on his lap, the audience will be surprised to see the limp form come to life.

MIDWAY ATTRACTIONS AND CONCESSIONS

Delighted as the guests will be with the main show of the three-ring circus, they will eagerly look forward to the announcement that the authentic, old-fashioned circus midway is open. The spirited music, the chants of the barkers with their "come-on" appeal to everyone, the colorful booths, and the banners will all lure the crowd to the area. The games may be set up on the ground, in simple booths, or on folding card tables. The booths can be very simple as illustrated on page 117.

You may want to assign each participating group or family the responsibility of providing one or more booths featuring a game or concession. Each group should be responsible for gathering their own props and prizes, figuring out how to get business, and cleaning up afterwards. If this is a more informal and casual entertainment, scour the neighborhood for games; most families have something they will be willing to contribute to this part of the circus.

Whether or not you charge for participating in each game depends on how you set up your admission fee. (See page 116.) It is perfectly logical to make a nominal charge for each game if money-making is your goal. If you are entertaining in your own back yard for a small group such as the neighborhood or a club or church group, forget the toll charge and use fewer concessions.

Any hard-surfaced area such as a tennis court, play area, or a drive-way is a good place to set up the midway and you can line both sides with booths. If it is necessary to use the lawn area, you should realize that the traffic *may* be damaging to the lawn. If the circus is held indoors, you can set up your arcade across one wall or the back of the hall.

If the crowd is large, you will want to control the flow of traffic to prevent congestion around certain areas. This may be done by issuing different colored tickets (stapled together, or in book form, or strip tickets as illustrated on page 122) for each attraction. If a very large crowd is expected, group the tickets in varying order so that tickets for one group of games are on top of some ticket books while they are near the bottom of others. This will prevent everyone from gathering at game number one and moving on to game number two as a group.

Prizes

Prizes can be given to the winners or to each contestant depending on your own desires. Suggestions for prizes for the games can be found on page 116. Another way to provide prizes is to collect "white elephants" (old toys, books, ornaments, jewelry—anything worthless) from your neighbors and friends. These may be wrapped as attractively as possible and the packages numbered so that the best will go to the one with the most points. If you have a generous supply of prizes such as gum, candies, and comic books, you may be able to give each contestant a prize at each game whether he wins or not. For those who do score high, special prizes can be awarded.

Following are some instructions for games and concessions that will be fairly simple to devise. The games and concessions can be adjusted or altered in name if you have a special theme to carry out or group to be honored. Relays and races will be fun for small children, but they are not included here.

If you have not provided other ways of dispensing your refreshments, then your food concessions featuring hotdogs, lemonade, popcorn, candy, and peanuts will fit in very well with the other midway attractions.

All set? Then how about trying your skill and luck at one of these games?

Flame Shoot

Set three lighted candles (plumber's candles are good for this or even "used" candles in various lengths) in candle holders on a table or platform. Give each guest three chances to shoot out the flames with a squirt gun. Give an extra turn for two hits out of three and a prize if a player douses them all. Experiment ahead of time to find the best shooting distance. Have extra candles and matches on hand. Protect your table from water by using an oil-cloth cover—it won't catch fire either!

Balloon Darts

Set a large piece of sturdy cardboard, wallboard, or plywood at the back of the booth or against a wall. Blow up and tie balloons, preferably small ones, and attach them to the board by sticking pins or thumbtacks through the stems. The contestants throw darts at the board trying to pop the balloons. Give five tries, and give prizes for three to five hits. For small children the distance from the throwing line to the dart board should be decreased; for older children and adults, it can be lengthened. You will need a good supply of balloons on hand to keep the board filled. However, remember that the game will only be challenging if you spread the balloons far enough apart; ten to twelve inches is about right if the balloons are small.

Bolo

This game, a favorite pastime in the Pampas, is constructed by tying two bright wooden spools with a stout cord so that the spools are on each end of the cord. A wooden frame resembling a lattice-work is set up. The cross pieces of the lattice are braced about twelve inches apart, and at each cross piece, a white circle with a number is fastened. Each player throws the bolo balls from a distance of 6 to 12 feet, trying to hit the cross piece and wind the bolo around it in order to score whatever number is there. Give prizes for the best scores.

Flying Saucer Game

To make a flying saucer, staple two 8-inch paper plates together, concave sides facing each other. This is thrown from a distance of ten or twelve feet at a target. The target can be a waste basket, grocery box, or a series of wire coat hangers suspended from a line. Score for each target hit. Give each contestant three tries at the target.

Bean Bag Toss

Make 4-inch square bean bags from sturdy fabric and fill them with beans, rice, or grain. These are to be tossed at a target such as a clown's face which has been painted on a piece of plywood or a grocery carton with eyes, nose, and mouth cut out. If the box is shallow depth, you can lean it against a wall so that the bean bags will fall to the bottom of the box and be easily retrieved. If the target is made from plywood, a stand can be attached to the back. The eyes, nose, and mouth can be labeled with different number values. The contestants' various scores should be added up and prizes awarded for high scores.

Back Yard Bowling

For this game a regulation softball, a croquet ball, or a sturdy rubber ball is rolled a distance of 12 to 20 feet. The target is a set of "ten pins" set up in regular bowling formation. Home-made "ten pins" can be made from wax milk cartons (partially filled with sand for ballast) or empty liquid detergent containers.

Snag a Nag

This game involves a stick horse and a lariat. The "horse" is made by stuffing a man's brown sock and tying it over a broom stick. Felt nose, eyes, and mouth can be appliqued on the stocking head if desired. The lariat is a length of rope which should be twirled around the head several times and then thrown to lasso the horse. Prizes are given to those who achieve this. You may want to substitute the "sawhorse" used in the bareback riding act for the stick horse.

Bell Ringer

A popular midway attraction is this device which attempts to measure strength. The "strong man" will be able to ring a bell with a swift and sturdy stroke of the mallet. Though the mechanism is not the easiest to make, the following suggestions might make it feasible for your midway: The lever is constructed from a 2" x 2" oak or maple board about 44 inches long which is reinforced in the center with a 2" x 4" board that is 12 inches long. It is pivoted near the center on a piece of half-inch pipe which has been drilled and bolted to the lever. The ends of the pipe are held firm in holes drilled halfway through side bracket blocks 2" x 4" x 6" which are in turn bolted to the 2" x 8" base. A rubber heel on the lever provides a target for the mallet. The weight slides on multistrand clothesline cable pulled taut by an eyebolt through the top. A tin can near the top of the wire clangs when the weight is hit high enough.

Shooting Gallery

If you do not wish to construct a booth for this concession, use a large packing case for the frame. Place a three-inch board across the front opening and set paper cups along the board. The contestant tries to hit the cups and knock them off the board with a play gun which shoots ping-pong balls. Six shots are standard for these ping-pong rifles. Prizes are awarded for good shooting.

Floating Saucers

Fill a metal laundry tub three-fourths full of water and float three small saucers in it. Mark a throwing line for patrons to stand on as they toss pennies or rubber washers at the saucers. Three hits out of five tries wins a prize.

Ring Toss

Make a pegboard and number each peg. Players throw rope rings or quoits at the pegs. A handicap may be set whereby the players must throw left-handed! If they're left-handed, then the right must be used.

Hit the Dodger

Paint a face on a large paper plate or piece of cardboard and cut out a round hole for the mouth. Fasten a string mesh bag or cloth bag behind the mouth to catch the balls. Fasten the face to an old sheet or canvas with the bag extending through a hole cut in the sheet. Or the face can be painted directly on a large piece of cardboard as illustrated with a bag fastened to the back to catch the balls. Give each customer three rubber balls to throw at this unpredictable face which is moved to and fro by the attendant.

Picture Gallery

Another kind of shooting gallery that your guests will enjoy is a picture-taking booth. Have someone with a polaroid camera take photographs in your picture gallery. On a large piece of cardboard or on an old sheet draw caricature figures making them unusual and funny. Cut out places where guests put their own heads and arms through. These pictures can be developed on the spot and sold for a nominal fee. If the gallery is indoors, be sure to provide several photo flood lamps.

Monocycle Ride

Give patrons a ride in an old-fashioned wheelbarrow!

Fish Pond

This is an all-time favorite with children and will be a real money maker if a nominal fee is charged! A special booth may be constructed for the fish pond or a doorway with a sheet hung across it may be used for the screened area. The workers stand behind the screen and attach prizes to the fishing pole tossed over by the eager children.

Weight Guessing

A small bathroom scale and someone who ad-libs cleverly are all you need for this favorite. A clown could very well take charge for all he has to do is try to guess the participant's weight within five pounds. If he misses, a prize is given. If you can enlist the assistance of a carpenter, you can make an extensive weight-guessing apparatus from a wooden tripod. Hang a strong scale (up to 300 pounds for safety) borrowed from your ice man or butcher from the tripod. From the hook end of the scale hang a light-weight chair such as an aluminum porch chair.

Fortune Telling

What's in the stars for you? Who can resist hearing about his future? Rig up a tent or booth for your fortune teller who wears a gypsy costume. Place a crystal ball (rose bowl or fish bowl turned upside down into which she can gaze with interest) on a table or, if you prefer, she can just read palms. Her speeches should not only be clever, but they should contain elements of suspense, extravagance, and surprise!

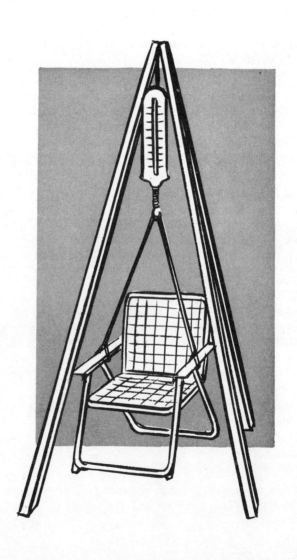

Pony Rides

If you have the space and can rent or borrow a Shetland pony or gentle horse, you can add a memorable feature to your circus carnival. Be sure a responsible person who understands horses is present to help the children mount and dismount and give assurance and guidance where needed.

Merry-Go-Round

A teeter-totter that revolves is sufficient for this attraction. However, if it is possible, rent or borrow one of the portable merry-go-rounds used as promotional aids by some business houses. These are described on page 124.

Well, there you have our ideas for a really entertaining neighborhood circus. We hope you try it sometime, and that *your* circus will be a rousing success.

ABOUT THE AUTHORS

SHIRLEY AND MONROE PAXMAN *are lifelong residents of Provo, Utah where Judge Paxman presides over the Juvenile Court. The parents of seven children, they share a deep appreciation for the values of family life and believe that the home where warmth, light-heartedness and loving-kindness are found will be a happy one. This and their other books represent only a part of the energies devoted by the Paxmans to the enrichment of family life everywhere.*

INDEX

189